dictatorship

mc Marshall Cavendish
Benchmark
New York

dictatorship

RON FRIDELL

Marshall   Cavendish   Benchmark
99 White Plains Road • Tarrytown,
NY 10591 • www.marshallcavendish.us
Copyright © 2008 by Marshall Cavendish
Corporation • Map Copyright © 2008 by
Marshall Cavendish Corporation • Map
by XNR Productions, Inc. • All rights
reserved. No part of this book may be
reproduced or utilized in any form or by
any means electronic or mechanical
including photocopying, recording, or by
any information storage and retrieval system,
without permission from the copyright
holders. • All Internet sites were available
and accurate when sent to press. • Fridell,
Ron. • Dictatorship / by Ron Fridell. •
p. cm. — (Political systems of the world) •
Summary: "Discusses dictatorships as
a political system, and details the • history
of dictatorships throughout the world"—
Provided by publisher. 8 Includes biblio-
graphical references and index. ISBN:
978-0-7614-2627-1 • 1. Dictatorship. 2.
Dictatorship—History. I. Title. • JC495.
F67 2007 • 321.9—dc22 • 2006023121

Photo research by Connie Gardner
Cover photo by Korea News Service/
Reuters/CORBIS • Photographs in this
book are used by permission and through
the courtesy of: *The Image Works:* Topham,
8; *The Granger Collection:* 12, 70, 118–119;
Corbis: Korean News Service/Reuters, 1, 3,
5, 6–7; Stapleton Collection, 14; Asian Art
and Archaeology, Inc., 21; Leonardo de
Selva, 25; Bettmann, 29, 66, 96; CORBIS,
44; Hulton-Deutsch Collection, 56; *Getty
Images:* AFP, 74; Ramzi Haidar/AFP, 114;
AP Photo: Ng Han Guan, 78; Pool, 102;
David Guttenfelder, 108.
Publisher: Michelle Bisson
Art Director: Anahid Hamparian
Series Designer: Sonia Chaghatzbanian
Printed in Malaysia
1 3 5 6 4 2

WITH THANKS TO ZOLTAN BARANY,
FRANK C. ERWIN JR. PROFESSOR
IN THE DEPARTMENT OF
GOVERNMENT AT THE UNIVERSITY
OF TEXAS, FOR HIS EXPERT
REVIEW OF THIS MANUSCRIPT.

Contents

dictatorship

Mao Zedong led the communist revolution in mainland China. For almost forty years, Chairman Mao had total control of the politics and economics of his vast nation.

The First Dictators

ONE DAY A VAST NATION'S ABSOLUTE ruler issued an urgent decree. All citizens were to join him in relentless pursuit of the terrible "four pests." Rats, sparrows, flies, and mosquitoes threatened the nation's health, he warned. But with all citizens working as one, these pests would be wiped away. Then the entire nation would take a great leap forward to become a healthier, happier place.

The state-controlled news media reported the early results. The response had been overwhelming. Millions had joined the hunt from every corner of the nation, and results were impressive.

The great leader's campaign had worked especially well against sparrows. Farm families were told to hurry out to their fields and bang pots and pans together and scream without stopping. When they did, the startled sparrows shot up into the air and stayed there while, far below, the banging and shouting continued. With nowhere to land, thousands of birds died in mid-air from exhaustion.

The leader was well-pleased with the people's response. Already the nation's health had improved—the environment too. One day in the near future, the leader proclaimed, the whole nation would become one vast garden.

DEADLY CONSEQUENCES

The leader was Mao Zedong, China's all-powerful dictator, and these events from the late 1950s were part of the Great Leap Forward, Mao's campaign to industrialize and modernize his nation. Sending millions of people out to render common pests extinct may sound irrational, but Chairman Mao was absolutely serious. With everyone working together, all things were possible, he believed, even the conquering of nature itself.

Mao was wrong. The dreaded four pests were not wiped away. Many sparrows died, though—with catastrophic consequences. Chairman Mao did not understand what a crucial part sparrows played in the balance of nature. These birds were voracious consumers of locusts. With so few sparrows remaining, a vast plague of locusts descended upon the land, ruining China's crops, and a nationwide famine killed millions.

DICTATORSHIP VERSUS DEMOCRACY

Events like these would not happen in a democratic nation, where no one person may take total charge, not even the head of state. Democracy is government by consent, with checks and balances limiting one and all. Power is shared among a number of elected leaders and restricted by a constitution and laws.

A dictatorship, on the other hand, is government by unrestricted decree. The dictator does not share power with a legislature or judiciary. He does not have to convince anyone that his plans are practical or even rational. He simply issues orders and watches the people do his bidding. His power is absolute and his decisions are law, no matter what harm they cause.

In a democracy, the state—at least ideally—exists for the benefit of its citizens. In a dictatorship, the citizens serve the state.

THE MODEST DICTATOR

Dictatorship is all about the use and misuse of personal power. Most of history's dictators are seen as tyrants: willful, cruel, destructive—and rightly so. Mao Zedong alone was held responsible for the death of tens of millions of innocent people.

But once upon a time in Ancient Rome, dictators were regarded with affection and admiration. The office of dictator originated there in 501 BCE

Ancient Rome was a republic. Its citizens chose their leaders, none of whom held absolute power. But in times of emergency, such as wars and rebellions, the Senate could appoint a dictator. His power was not absolute, though. His term of office ran for only six months, he did not control the public finances, and he was held strictly accountable for his conduct while in office.

Lucius Quinctius Cincinnatus has gone down in history as the ideal role model for the Roman dictator: a take-charge kind of man on the one hand and modest on the other. He served two terms, in 458 BCE and 439 BCE.

In his first six-month term as dictator, Cincinnatus helped turn back two tribes, the Volscians and the Aequi, who were menacing Rome. During his second term he helped put down a revolt by the plebeians, the people of Rome who did not belong to the privileged classes. On both occasions Cincinnatus promptly resigned when his term expired, or earlier, and returned to his life as a farmer.

His memory has lived on. When George Washington resigned after serving two terms as first president of the United States, choosing to step aside rather that seek more power, he was favorably compared to Cincinnatus.

THE TYRANNICAL DICTATOR

The same could not be said of Gaius Julius Caesar. Rome had eighty-eight dictators in all and Caesar was the last—for good reason. He was not the first Roman politician who used his position to gain more control of the government, but Caesar was the first to attempt to turn himself into Rome's ruler for life.

Caesar was born into a wealthy family in 100 BCE. In 59 BCE he was elected senior consul of the Roman Republic, the equivalent of president, for a one-year term. Then he embarked on a series of empire-building military campaigns in Gaul, modern-day France; Britannia, modern-day Britain; and Egypt. A likeness of his face appeared on Roman coins, and he was said to proclaim, "Rem Publicam sum!"—"I am the Republic!"

Caesar's glory grew to such heights that he was proclaimed Dictator Perpetuus, dictator for life, in 45 BCE. Never had a Roman leader enjoyed such power. One day, when he was visited by a senatorial delegation, he made a fatal mistake. Caesar should have risen when the senators approached him as a way of showing them proper respect. By refusing to rise, Caesar insulted them deeply.

Now, instead of respect and admiration, Caesar was inspiring dread

Gaius Julius Caesar wanted to rule Rome for life. Instead, he was murdered by Roman nobles, including Brutus and Cassius, at the Roman Senate on the Ides of March, March 15, 44 BCE.

and dislike. Here was a man with the power to do as he pleased acting as though he were above the rest of Rome—a tyrant in their midst. In 44 BCE, a group of senators surrounded him, drew their knives and swords, and assassinated their arrogant dictator.

Caesar's misuse of power led the Roman Senate to abolish the office of dictator forever. But that hasn't stopped dictators and dictatorships from springing up in nations all around the world, right up to the present day.

GENGISKAN,
Grand Mogol.
Tiré en partie de la Voix Salomon).

Paris chez Duflos rue St Victor

A.P.D.R.

Genghis Khan expanded his Mongolian empire to include much of Asia, slaughtering millions in his conquest of foreign lands.

2
From Khan to Díaz ■ ■ ■

THE MANY DICTATORS WHO HAVE RISEN TO POWER throughout history have gotten there in different ways. Genghis Khan got there on the back of a horse.

Julius Caesar was born into wealth and privilege and destined for a career in the military and politics, but not Genghis Khan. Khan was born into extreme poverty in the steppes region of Mongolia in about 1162.

Caesar's life was well-documented by historians of the time, but few primary-source records exist about the life and times of Genghis Khan. Much of what follows comes from legend and lore handed down by word of mouth through the years.

At birth, the boy who would become Genghis Khan was given the name Temüjin, meaning "blacksmith." Temüjin grew up in a land of warring tribes and clans. As a young man he became his clan's leader and led his warriors on to conquer neighboring clans. Temüjin kept expanding his empire relentlessly until, by 1206, he was known as Genghis Khan, or "Oceanic Ruler." He had united the various tribes into one tribe, the Mongols.

But that was not enough. The charismatic Khan then ventured, alternately, westward toward Europe and eastward toward China to create one of the greatest land empires in history.

HORSE SOLDIERS

The steppes are vast, flat expanses of grassland in Northern Asia with a scattering of lakes, forests, and mountains. It's a harsh environment but a rich one. Now, as then, nomads herd reindeer, yak, sheep, goats—and horses.

Mongolian horses have always been short and stubby. Next to horses from the American West, they appear inferior, poorly bred. But Genghis Khan knew how to use their small size to tactical advantage. He and his horse soldiers, who rode bareback to lighten their horses' loads, could easily and quickly leap on and off their low-to-the-ground mounts in battle.

Khan was known as an organizational genius who created one of the most highly disciplined armies in history. He was also a keen military strategist. For a cavalry, rivers may present difficult, even insurmountable, obstacles. But during a winter invasion of Russia, Khan used the frozen rivers like smooth, clear roads, to surprise and defeat the enemy.

On another occasion his army could not penetrate the walls surrounding Ningxia, capital of the vast Chinese state of Xi Xia, which comprised much of northwestern China and parts of Tibet. So Khan had his men divert water from a nearby canal. Soon a flood hit the city, and the inhabitants of Ningxia were forced to surrender. By the year 1210 Khan and his armies had conquered Xi Xia.

Genghis Khan and his armies had well-earned reputations as merciless warriors, sometimes fighting not just to conquer but to exact revenge for a past defeat or insult. In 1215 they conquered the city of Zhongdu, the location now occupied by China's capital of Beijing. Khan's tactic was simple. His army starved Zhongdu's inhabitants until they gave up. Then Khan's men looted the city.

During a series of battles in 1219–1220, after defeating the cities of Bokhara, Samarkand, and Balkh, Khan's army burned each one to the ground. These cities were part of the Khwarazmian empire in Central Asia, which included today's Uzbekistan. From 1219 to 1222, the Mongols swept across this vast empire and added it to their own. Estimates of the total number of deaths from Khan's armies run into the millions.

GRAND EXPECTATIONS

As his empire grew, Khan established a transcontinental mail service to communicate across vast spaces. At its height, Genghis Khan's land empire was the largest the world had ever seen, stretching all the way from Asia's Aral Sea to the Yellow Sea of China.

Genghis Khan had succeeded in uniting Mongolia and expanding it into a vast kingdom. But was it vast enough to satisfy Khan's god-like vision of himself? As a young man, Khan already felt chosen for monumental purposes: "My strength was fortified by Heaven and Earth," he was quoted as saying. And later in life: "I am the punishment of God" and "If you had not committed great sins, God would not have sent a punishment like me upon you."

A MYSTERIOUS DEATH

Khan died in 1227. Even after death, his word was still law. Legend says that Khan had left orders to keep his passing cloaked in secrecy. No one but his heirs were to know where the body lay buried.

To carry out Khan's orders, soldiers were said to have killed each of the 2,500 people who were unfortunate enough to have witnessed the funeral procession. And when those soldiers returned from the burial, they too were executed.

After Khan's death, his kingdom was turned over to his four sons, Jochi, Ogodei, Chaghatai, and Tolui. They then led the Mongol armies further into the Middle East, Eastern Europe, and China, adding to their father's fabled kingdom.

Khan's body was buried in an unmarked grave. People still mount expeditions into Inner Mongolia, now part of the People's Republic of China, to hunt for Khan's elusive remains.

LORENZO THE MAGNIFICENT

Dictators are ambitious by nature. Like Caesar, they crave power. Like Khan, they hold grand expectations. Both men rose to power through military might. Other dictators have relied on gentler, more psychological skills.

Lorenzo di Piero de Medici was the unofficial dictator of the city of Florence during the Italian Renaissance. Though he ran the affairs of the city from 1469 until his death in 1492, Lorenzo never took on any official title. During those years, wrote sixteenth century historian Francesco Guicciardini, "it would not have been possible for Florence to have had a better or a more pleasant tyrant."

Lorenzo the Magnificent, as he was known, also had a dark side. But he is better remembered as a lively, kind, and generous man who patronized his city's brilliant artists. Lorenzo was born into Florence's leading banking family and its vast wealth, much of which he used to fund the work of Leonardo da Vinci, Michelangelo, Botticelli, and other Renaissance painters and sculptors.

REVENGE AND DIPLOMACY

At this time Northern Italy was a loose collection of five chief city-states that were often at odds, making secret alliances and conspiring against one another. One of these alliances was forged among the Archbishop of Pisa, Pope Sixtus IV, and a powerful rival of the Medicis, the Pazzi family.

In 1478 the three conspired to assassinate Lorenzo and his brothers. The Pazzi family would do the dirty work. This would please the pope and the archbishop, who had grown uncomfortable with Lorenzo's growing power. Then the Pazzis would take charge and assume secular leadership of Florence.

The coup attempt took place during Easter Sunday Mass in the Cathedral of Santa Maria del Fiore. One of Lorenzo's brothers was stabbed to death and Lorenzo himself was badly wounded.

As Lorenzo recovered from his wounds, his supporters got him his revenge. They methodically tracked down the entire Pazzi family and killed them all. The archbishop also met his end, by hanging at the end of a rope.

Then the Medici supporters prepared to execute the pope's nephew, but Lorenzo stepped in. The nephew was not in on the conspiracy, he insisted, and saving him should win the powerful pope's gratitude.

But no, the pope plotted revenge through a military alliance with the King of Naples. When the Medicis learned of the plot, they saw disaster looming. But Lorenzo took matters in hand by abruptly switching roles from aggrieved avenger to diplomat and peacemaker. He traveled to Naples, where he met with the king and came away with an agreement not to go to war with Florence.

POWER AND PEACE

This feat of diplomacy made Lorenzo even more popular with the Florentines. He used this newfound admiration to his advantage, securing changes to the state's constitution that further enhanced his power. After that he pursued a policy of peace with Florence's rival states. It was a difficult balancing act with so many secret alliances and

The Prince

Florentine author Niccolo Machiavelli wrote *The Prince* for Lorenzo the Magnificent's family, the Medicis, hoping to secure their favor. In this classic treatise on the acquisition and use of political power, the author advises a ruling prince on how he can best use war and a ruthless attitude to maintain a strong and stable government. When political scholars analyze statecraft today, they often speak of "Machiavellian thinking." Here are some examples:

On the use of force versus law:
"You must know there are two ways of [fighting], the one by the law, the other by force; the first method is proper to men, the second to beasts; but because the first is frequently not sufficient, it is necessary to have recourse to the second. Therefore it is necessary for a prince to understand how to avail himself of the beast and the man."

On weapons and allies:
"[A] prince ought to have two fears, one from within, on account of his subjects, the other from without, on account of external powers. From the latter he is defended by being well armed and having good allies, and if he is well armed he will have good friends . . ."

On why it is safer for a prince to be feared than loved: "[M]en have less scruple in offending one who is beloved than one who is feared, for love is preserved by the link of obligation which, owing to the baseness of men, is broken at every opportunity for their advantage; but fear preserves you by a dread of punishment which never fails."

conspiracies constantly in the works, but Lorenzo's skills as a deal-maker and diplomat kept the peace intact.

Lorenzo the Magnificent fell short of his ultimate goal, though: the unification of Italy. After his death, in 1492, the tenuous peace between the five northern Italian states fell apart. Two years later the French invaded, and for the next four hundred years the Italian peninsula would be occupied by foreign powers.

TOYOTOMI HIDEYOSHI

In 1536, Japan's Toyotomi Hideyoshi was born into a country that, for the past two hundred years, had been wracked with civil war. No centralized government existed to take control. Rival clans kept fighting each other, and the peasants kept revolting against the upper classes. As a result, Japan had no lasting peace and no unified system of laws. Bandits roamed the countryside, preying on travelers. And the nation was largely cut off from the rest of the world.

Hideyoshi rose to power as a military leader in one of these warring clans. Like Genghis Khan, he had a knack for inventing ingenious ways to win battles. In 1582 he was confronted with an especially imposing task: to take the fortress known as Takamatsu Castle and the powerful army within.

First he tried bribery, but Shimiazu Muneharu, captain of the forces inside the castle, would have none of that. Attempts to take the fortress by force also failed. After sizing up the difficult situation and the surrounding terrain, Hideyoshi decided on a most elaborate and unconventional plan.

Takamatsu lay on a flat plain just below sea level. The Ashimorigawa River ran nearby. Hideyoshi ordered it dammed. As his army dug up the land around the castle, the rising waters flowed in around it.

Soon Takamatsu had been turned into a castle island, isolated in the middle of a lake. Then, Hideyoshi's army commenced a campaign of constant bombardment with rifle and cannon fire. It was only a matter of time before the cornered enemy forces surrendered.

UNITY AND REFORM

Hideyoshi kept winning battles and gathering power and honor. In 1582 he was named civilian dictator and in 1585 the emperor gave him the title of *kampaku*, or imperial regent. Hideyoshi had been

Sixteenth century Toyotomi Hideyoshi was portrayed as having godlike powers. In this print, Hideyoshi is caught in a supernatural thunderstorm, but remains calm even though his attendants panic.

born a peasant. No one of peasant rank had ever achieved such a high office. But Hideyoshi's aims went well beyond the personal. His driving ambition was to unify Japan.

With this goal in mind, in 1588, Hideyoshi used his dictatorial powers to declare a national sword hunt. All peasants were forced to surrender their swords. This meant a sacrifice of individual freedom, since peasants were now forbidden to own weapons. But it also meant a step toward peace. There would be no more peasant revolts in Japan.

Hideyoshi also ordered an extensive survey of the entire nation, including a census. Once all citizens were registered, the government knew where everyone lived.

Now Hideyoshi could issue another order: Citizens had to get official permission to leave their provinces. Again, some freedom was sacrificed and some gained. Warring clans were no longer free to battle one another, nor could bandits roam the countryside at will.

Hideyoshi's other reforms included abolishing slavery and setting up a new system of government that equalized power between the rival warlords, or *daimyo*. He also encouraged foreign trade. The result was a more peaceful and prosperous nation.

WAR AND PEACE

Outside the nation, though, things were far from peaceful. Hideyoshi launched two military campaigns through the Korean peninsula toward China. Both wars were savage and unsuccessful. Hideyoshi's ambitions had exceeded his abilities.

It was the wrong time for war in Japan. Not that the country was short of weapons. No nation possessed more guns and cannons. But thanks in large part to Hideyoshi, Japan knew peace for the first time in 250 years. The Japanese people wanted to enjoy this peace that their dictator had brought them, not make war on other nations.

Hideyoshi died in 1598. On his orders, power passed along to his son, Hideyori. But the boy was underage and quickly lost claim to the power his father had held. Hideyoshi's long-time adversary, Tokugawa Ieyasu, then ascended to power in his place. But Tokugawa respected his rival, and many of Hideyoshi's reforms lived long after him.

NAPOLEON BONAPARTE

Napoleon Bonaparte was twenty years old in 1789 when the French Revolution erupted. Causes included high unemployment, low food supplies, and a long-running resentment of the absolute rule of the very many by the very few.

In the tumultuous decade that followed, France would evolve from an absolute monarchy, ruled by kings and queens, into the fragile beginnings of a republic mostly run by the citizens of the nation.

The Revolution would end in 1799 when a military dictator took charge, bringing a temporary end to hopes for a true republic. Five years later this dictator would become emperor, and eleven years after that, in 1814, he would lose his power. It would be hard to find a more extreme and dramatic rise and fall than that of Napoleon Bonaparte.

THE LITTLE CORPORAL

The key to Napoleon's rise was being in the right place at the right time. The year was 1795, and Royalists were on the attack. These counter-revolutionaries wanted to turn France back into an absolute monarchy. Their target was the constitutional convention taking place at the Tuileries Palace in Paris.

Napoleon, who had achieved a modest position of command in the French army, was there to defend the forces of the revolution from the forces of counter-revolution. His strategy was simple and effective. He used artillery to clear the streets of royalists with what he called a "whiff of grapeshot": cloth bags stuffed with musket balls fired from cannons, a devastating anti-personnel weapon.

This dramatic victory brought Napoleon wealth and fame, but more importantly for him, power. He was put in command of the French army, which a year later he led into Italy. The successful invasion earned him the affectionate nickname *le petit corporal*, the little corporal, bestowed upon him by his grateful troops.

TO EGYPT AND BACK

From there it was on to Egypt in 1798, where Napoleon's 34,000-man army faced the Mamelukes, who had ruled Egypt for seven centuries. This fierce warrior caste was famous for its agile and powerful cavalry, while the French had hardly any horse soldiers. Yet Napoleon's forces won handily.

One key to victory was a tactic called hollow squares. Napoleon organized his soldiers into groups facing outward in all directions. From this formation the troops could repel a cavalry attack from any side while simultaneously protecting the supplies and ammunition at their backs, inside the square. Napoleon's forces won the Battle of the Pyramids, so named for its location, about 4 miles (6.4 kilometers) from the Pyramids of Giza. Only 300 French troops were reported killed, versus 6,000 Mamelukes.

Napoleon returned to France in 1799 and found both trouble and good fortune. The young republic was bankrupt. Napoleon saw a golden opportunity and seized it. Using troops under his command, he staged a coup and seized power. All hopes for a lasting republic seemed dashed when Napoleon assumed power as First Consul, making himself the equivalent of a military dictator.

HIS GREATEST ACHIEVEMENT

But Napoleon then instituted a broad series of reforms designed to further France's evolution toward a republic. He centralized the government and organized it into departments. He reformed the tax, banking, educational, road, and sewer systems.

Most importantly, he reformed the nation's legal system in line with the ideals of the French Revolution. Before Napoleon's reforms, laws varied from place to place according to local customs. There were more than 400 separate codes of laws in operation throughout France. And instead of all citizens being treated equally, certain people still benefited from exemptions and privileges granted by France's kings and queens decades ago.

Napoleon's new set of laws, the Napoleonic Code or Civil Code, changed all that. Now one set of clearly written laws applied to all citizens. The Civil Code would serve as the model for future codes of law in more than twenty nations. Later in life Napoleon would call the code his greatest achievement.

THE EMPEROR AND EXILE

The codes were approved in 1804, the same year that Napoleon was elected First Consul for life. That same year he took the next step toward absolute power by declaring himself emperor. Pope Pius VII

Napoleon Bonaparte started as a soldier of the French Revolution and, five years later, declared himself emperor of France.

crowned him on December 2, 1804, in Paris's Notre Dame Cathedral.

For the next ten years Napoleon the emperor led the armies of France eastward and southward to conquer more and more of Europe. But Russia proved his undoing. He won the battle, leading his troops into Moscow, but he lost the war.

The harsh Russian winter beat him, that and Russia's scorched earth tactic. As they retreated from the French, the Russians destroyed anything and everything that might be of use to the enemy, especially food. They burned crops and slaughtered livestock. They even burned their capital city to the ground. A long way from home, the French had little to eat during the long winter.

Meanwhile, Britain, Spain, and Portugal joined Russia and the German states in a coalition against France. The Allies surrounded Napoleon's nation and his weakened army. Then they invaded and captured Paris in 1814.

Napoleon ended his life in exile, a man alone on the tiny island of St. Helena, off the western coast of Africa, where he died in 1821. In 1841 his body was taken back to Paris and buried there, in the city where he had once been crowned emperor of France and its European empire.

During his years of power, Napoleon had taken France on a dizzying political ride from a budding republic to a military dictatorship to an absolute monarchy. After Napoleon's fall in 1815, France settled back into monarchy.

PORFIRIO DÍAZ

Porfirio Díaz was born in Oaxaca, Mexico, in 1830. As a young man, he was destined to become a champion of Mexico's poor and downtrodden, opposing the power of the rich and privileged.

Díaz was just sixteen when he joined a local militia to help protect Mexico from a possible U.S. invasion. Later on, he rose through army ranks to become commander. Then he took part in a plan to overthrow Mexico's dictator, Santa Anna.

The plan worked. Santa Anna fled the country in 1855. Events moved quickly after that. Within two years a new constitution led to a civil war. After that war another war erupted. By the end of the second war, in 1867, Díaz's military skills had brought him fame, while his

Napoleon's Farewell

After Paris fell to the Allies in 1814, Napoleon gathered together the men who had served in his army the longest and expressed his deep feelings for them. Here is an English translation of that farewell speech:

Soldiers of my Old Guard: I bid you farewell. For twenty years I have constantly accompanied you on the road to honor and glory. In these latter times, as in the days of our prosperity, you have invariably been models of courage and fidelity. With men such as you our cause could not be lost; but the war would have been interminable; it would have been civil war, and that would have entailed deeper misfortunes on France.

I have sacrificed all of my interests to those of the country. I go, but you, my friends, will continue to serve France. Her happiness was my only thought. It will still be the object of my wishes. Do not regret my fate; if I have consented to survive, it is to serve your glory. I intend to write the history of the great achievements we have performed together. Adieu, my friends. Would I could press you all to my heart.

liberal politics had made him an admired figure among Mexico's poor. Then came the event that lifted Díaz to power.

LAW AND ORDER

Another revolt shook Mexico in 1876, with Díaz a leader of the rebels. Again he was instrumental in unseating a dictator, President Sebastián Lerdo de Tejada. This time it led him to the presidency. Díaz was elected on a platform of democratic reforms to help the poor.

His reform program focused on foreign investment and law and order. Mexico needed foreign investment from the United States to modernize the country and raise standards of living, but in order to gain foreign investors, Mexico first had to establish domestic peace. Like Hideyoshi's Japan, Díaz's Mexico had been racked with civil wars as warlords fought one another and packs of bandits roamed the countryside.

How would he bring law and order out of lawlessness and chaos? Díaz created an entity that many dictators rely on for internal security, a brutal police force run by and for their leader. Díaz was known for his cunning and his skills at manipulating people. For his new lawmen, he turned to Mexico's bandit population.

These bandits became the hard core of Díaz's rural police, or *rurales*, a paramilitary force far better trained, equipped, and paid than the soldiers Díaz had commanded, and with a far more brutal reputation. The bandit problem went away almost at once, and the rurales stood ever ready to put down any attempt at a peasant revolt.

UPS AND DOWNS

To help him remain in office, Díaz had the constitution amended to lift all restrictions on the number of terms the president could serve. Officially, Díaz was Mexico's president, but in reality he was its dictator. Díaz controlled Mexico from 1876 until 1911. (From 1880–1884, he was out of office but still in absolute control.) To remain in power all those years, Díaz resorted to bribes, election fraud, and violence from his rurales, which included assassination of opponents.

History gives Díaz credit for rapidly modernizing Mexico, thanks in part to increased investment from the United States. He helped create an urban working class by encouraging the construction of factories in Mexico City. Statistics tell the story. Under his rule, the

President Porfirio Díaz was officially president of Mexico, but was really its dictator from 1876 to 1911, at which time the Mexican Revolution began.

amount of railroad track in the nation increased from just about zero to 8,700 miles (14,000 kilometers). Silver production tripled and copper production jumped 800 percent.

But another set of statistics tells a different story. As of 1895, a Mexican citizen could expect to live only to the age of thirty. A 1900 survey classified 16 percent of the Mexican population as homeless, and a 1910 census declared 50 percent of all Mexican houses to be unfit for human habitation. Under Díaz, wealth increased for a few but not for the many whom Díaz had once championed. The majority of the population still lived in poverty.

Díaz's reign as dictator ended shortly after he declared himself the landslide winner in an election that many believed should have gone to his opponent, Francisco Madero, whom Díaz had jailed before the election. Díaz's massive vote fraud led to a revolt, which forced him to flee into exile.

As Díaz sailed across the Atlantic Ocean bound for France in 1911, back in his native country, the Mexican Revolution had begun. Warlords and their armies would fight each other for another six years. Then would come the Constitution of 1917 and with it, a step toward democracy for the Mexican people.

3
Two Kinds of Dictators ■ ■ ■

BY DEFINITION, ALL DICTATORSHIPS ARE AUTHORITARIAN. The dictator demands obedience to his authority over any desire for individual freedom. It is the dictator alone, not the individual citizen or elected representative, who determines what's right and wrong and what's best for the nation.

Theocracies and absolute monarchies are authoritarian governments as well, but they are not dictatorships. In a theocracy, the government leaders are also the religious leaders, ruling as representatives of a deity. By contrast, dictatorships are run by secular leaders. In an absolute monarchy, the king or queen attains power by inheritance, and this can happen in a dictatorship as well. After Genghis Khan's death, his sons took over leadership of the Mongolian empire. But that was by Khan's choice, not by any hard-and-fast rule of succession.

Many dictators come to power by force, often backed by the nation's military forces. Napoleon gained power by a military coup. Other dictators, such as Díaz, were voted into office in fair and open elections or gained and kept power through a combination of force and rigged elections.

AUTHORITY AND STRUCTURE
To enforce his authority and carry out his orders, the authoritarian dictator must have a structured administration of some kind. In

the case of the legendary Genghis Khan, it might have been just a simple military chain of command. Khan and his armies were nearly always on the move. For civilian dictator Lorenzo the Magnificent, an informal network of relatives and well-connected friends served as his administration.

For Caesar, Hideyoshi, Napoleon, and Díaz, it was a formal bureaucracy with various offices and departments devoted to typical governmental tasks, such as administering the nation's finances, running its educational system, and constructing and maintaining its roads. The people who head up the departments in the bureaucracy are usually an inner circle of the dictator's close friends and colleagues, people he can trust to carry out his orders. In the cases of Caesar and Napoleon, there were also elected legislators who were bound to obey their leader's orders. Many dictators also keep a feared private police force, such as Porfirio Díaz's rurales, to enforce their authority.

TOTAL CONTROL

Typical authoritarian dictatorships are conservative by nature. The dictator's main concerns are gathering more power and remaining in control. Like Hideyoshi and Napoleon, they may work to improve things, but they are not out to revolutionize the basic structure of society.

Another kind of dictatorship is revolutionary by nature. This extreme form of government, totalitarianism, came into being during the twentieth century. As the name suggests, totalitarian governments aim to drastically alter society and to maintain total control over all aspects of daily life, including the behavior and beliefs of its citizens.

Totalitarian regimes base their revolution on an ideology, a system of beliefs that professes to explain the world and how to change it. Whatever the ideology, it claims to hold the answers to questions that have puzzled people throughout human history, the knowledge of the mysterious laws that supposedly govern the universe. "This is the way people and history work," the totalitarian dictator says. "Together we can transform human nature and remake our nation and the world."

HITLER'S "-ISMS"

Adolf Hitler was Germany's totalitarian dictator from 1933–1945. During that time he transformed German society, built a European empire, and was responsible for the deaths of millions of innocent people. He was guided by the ideology of Naziism, or National Socialism, a volatile concoction of fascism and racialism.

In the political philosophy of fascism, the individual exists to serve the state. A strong centralized government exercises tight control over economic and social activities. The national government owns and controls major industries. At the head is a dictator who promotes an extreme brand of nationalism.

Hitler's Naziism would lead the German people into becoming the aggressors in World War II, with an ultimate goal of world domination. Victory was inevitable, Hitler insisted, because history was inevitable and he knew right where history was headed.

Here was where the ideology of racialism came into play. According to Hitler, history was the unfolding of a series of battles based on human racial characteristics. Some races were strong, others were weak, and only the strong would survive.

SURVIVAL OF THE FITTEST

Hitler's race-based ideology stemmed from a twisted misinterpretation of the writings of Charles Darwin. In 1859, Darwin published his revolutionary book *On The Origin of Species*, a scientific study explaining how life originated and developed over the past several billion years. During Hitler's time, Darwin's book and ideas were widely circulated and accepted in Europe.

Darwin's explanation focuses on two broad ideas. His theory of evolution traces how living things have evolved, or developed, from one form to another through time. *Homo sapiens*, for example, evolved from ape species. Millions of years ago, one branch of the ape family developed into humans, while the other branches continued to develop as apes.

Darwin's other big idea is known as survival of the fittest. It explains how species have developed through a process of trial and error called random genetic mutation. Cells contain genes, which govern how all living things function and develop. From time to time, the genetic material in the cells of a living thing randomly change, altering the plant's or animal's characteristics. For instance, a random mutation might cause certain dogs to be born with a keener sense of smell than their fellow canines.

If these random mutations prove to be positive, they will be passed along from generation to generation. Positively mutated plants and animals tend to thrive, while those without these helpful mutations tend to die out and become extinct. Gradually, through vast stretches of time, only the fittest species inhabit the Earth. Species with positive adaptations survive; those without perish.

DARWIN MISINTERPRETED

Darwin's ideas are grounded in science. They concern the evolution of plant and animal species over vast amounts of time: millions, tens of millions, even billions of years. Those ideas were never meant to apply to the social and historical development of human societies.

Some people ignored this time factor and twisted Darwin's ideas to suit their aim of developing a human master race. These misinterpretations became known as Social Darwinism, a social theory that sees human history as an ongoing combat, with the strong inevitably surviving and the weak eventually dying out.

To hasten this process, racially superior men would father children only with racially superior women, while the inferior races would have no children at all. They would be sterilized and eventually die out.

Eugenics was the name given to this program of selective breeding. The term was first popularized by an English scientist, inventor, and mathematician, Sir Francis Galton, a half-cousin of Darwin's. In 1892 Galton wrote, "I wish again to emphasize the fact that the improvement of the natural gifts of future generations of the human race is largely, though indirectly, under our control. We may not be able to originate, but we can guide. The processes of evolution are in constant and spontaneous activity, some pushing towards the bad, some towards the good. Our part is to watch for opportunities to intervene by checking the former and giving free play to the latter."

EUGENICS

The early supporters of eugenics meant no harm. Their intentions were to make the entire human race healthier and more intelligent. The harm lay in the methods used to realize those good intentions.

At first, supporters of eugenics simply urged people who were mentally and physically fit to have lots of children. They did not advocate taking away anyone's right to have children.

But as eugenics became more accepted, people started advocating laws to prevent "unfit" people from breeding. They included those who had committed violent crimes, who were mentally ill, or who had learning disorders.

Eugenics' popularity was not confined to Europe. In the United States, some states passed laws that allowed doctors to sterilize people classified as unfit. Many Americans agreed with these laws. Among them was Theodore Roosevelt, the twenty-sixth president of the United States (1901–1909), who declared, "[T]he prime duty, the inescapable duty, of the good citizen of the right type is to leave his or her blood behind him in the world." Supreme Court Justice Oliver Wendell Holmes, who served on the Court from 1902–1932, agreed: "We want people who are healthy, good-natured, emotionally stable, sympathetic, and smart. We do not want idiots, imbeciles, paupers, and criminals."

By the 1930s, these eugenics-based laws had led to more than 100,000 people in the United States being sterilized against their will. More would have suffered the same fate if not for the horrific events taking place in Europe, which brought the eugenics movement to an end everywhere but in Hitler's Nazi Germany.

4
Hitler's Grand Plan

ADOLF HITLER'S RISE TO POWER began in the 1920s, when Germany was still reeling from its unexpected and humiliating defeat in World War I (1914–1918). That defeat came at the hands of the Allied Powers, which included France, Britain, and the United States.

The Versailles Treaty of June 28, 1919, settled the war. Leaders representing 75 percent of the world's population attended the peace conference at which the treaty was negotiated. The proceedings were dominated by the five Allied powers responsible for defeating Germany and the other Central Powers: the United States, Great Britain, France, Italy, and Japan.

As punishment, Germany had to give in to Allied demands. It was forced to surrender some of its national territory, such as the Alsace-Lorraine region, which went to France, and all of its overseas colonies. Much of the German army, navy, and air force was forced to disband. The nation also had to formally admit its guilt in starting the war and pursuing a policy of aggression and to pay millions of dollars to the Allied victors in reparation. As a result, Germany's borders shrank and its pride and economy were devastated.

Germany's ruling government after the defeat was the Weimar Republic. Named after the new capital city of Weimar, this was Germany's first-ever parliamentary democracy. It was not a well-liked government. Many of the German people saw it as weak because it was forced to give in to Allied demands and because the German economy was in such dire straits. A once strong and ambitious nation striding boldly towards power was now a weak and humbled country stumbling backward into oblivion.

HITLER'S CONCERNS

Not all Germans blamed the war's victors for their problems, but many did, including Hitler. For the past fifty years, the German people had been put through sweeping changes while struggling to adjust to Europe's Industrial Revolution, which Hitler also blamed on the Allies. In his view, the Industrial Revolution had radically changed life in Germany—and not for the better.

Hitler saw the changes from rural farm life to big city industrial life as soul-destroying. Instead of good, simple lives as farmers, more and more Germans now lived poor, anxious lives slaving away in big-city factories run by rich and greedy capitalists. As a young man, Hitler wrote:

> [T]he weekly wage is used up by the whole family in two or three days; they eat and drink as long as the money holds out and the last days they go hungry. Then the wife drags herself out into the neighborhood, borrows a little, runs up little debts at the food store, and in this way strives to get through the hard last days of the week. At noon they all sit together before their meager and sometimes empty bowls, waiting for the next payday, speaking of it, making plans, and, in their hunger, dreaming of the happiness to come. And so the little children, in their earliest beginnings, are made familiar with this misery.

Hitler's early writings show compassion for people who suffered economic hardship, as he himself had suffered growing up. If Hitler had been a different sort of person, that compassion might have led him to help the poor. Instead, it helped fuel a vengeful hatred of those he blamed for Germany's economic and military misfortunes.

THE THIRD REICH

Hitler had fought in World War I, and he took Germany's defeat hard. It stirred in him a driving mixture of envy, jealousy, and resentment— and a powerful longing for revenge.

His urge for vengeance was fanned by the flames of nationalism. In the 1920s, the German people reacted to their World War I defeat with a surge of nationalistic passion. They felt they must gain back the territory lost in the war—and more. They must bring all German-speaking people living in European nations together into a nation of their own. "One blood demands one Reich," Hitler wrote.

Reich is the German word for "empire." Rather than feeling humbled by defeat, Hitler felt enraged and aggressive, and many other Germans shared his feelings. Germany had been an empire twice before. The Holy Roman Empire (962–1806) was the First Reich; the Hohenzollern Empire (1871–1919) was the Second Reich. Now they thought it was time to rise up and make a Third Reich.

PRISON TIME

When a gang of unemployed soldiers started the Nazi Party in 1919, few thought it would one day become Germany's ruling government. Hitler joined early on and by 1921 had taken over party leadership.

At that point he assumed the title of *Fuhrer*, German for leader, guide, and chief. The word also suggested the idea of a prophet who would decisively lead his people into a bright and glorious future.

Hitler became leader thanks largely to his ability to deliver fiery speeches highlighting the faults of the existing government and the burning need for change. The members of Germany's weak post-war government were traitors to the nation for surrendering to the Allies, Hitler declared. They had to be overthrown.

By 1923, Nazi membership was at 55,000 and growing. They were the biggest and best organized of the parties opposing the Weimar Republic, and members were demanding action. Hitler knew that if he wanted to remain the party leader, he would have to act, so he hatched a plot.

The city of Munich in the German state of Bavaria was a hotbed of opposition to the Republic. The Nazis planned to kidnap the Bavarian government leaders as they gathered in a Munich beer hall and hold them at gunpoint until they agreed to accept Hitler as their leader.

The Nazis made their move on November 9, 1923, in the Beer Hall Putsch, or coup. Throughout the long night, Hitler and his storm troopers threatened the Bavarian political leaders gathered in the hall and German soldiers housed in barracks nearby. The plot unraveled, though, and Hitler landed in jail.

A Determined
Young Man

According to Hitler's writings, his youth was troubled. At home there was poverty. At school there was strife. But he refused to let these obstacles get him down, he wrote. Instead, he used them to prepare himself for leadership.

The seeds of Hitler's undeniably powerful skills as a speaker were planted in clashes at school. "I believe that even my oratorical talent was being developed in the form of . . . violent arguments with my schoolmates. I had become a little ringleader," he wrote.

Reading books on war from his father's library planted the seeds of his lifelong passion for conflict. When he read them, Hitler wrote, "I became more and more enthusiastic about everything that was in any way connected with war."

As a young man, Hitler developed the ability to turn strife into strength. "While the Goddess of Suffering took me in her arms, often threatening to crush me, my will to resistance grew, and in the end this will was victorious."

Hitler's prison time was not wasted. His cellmate was colleague Rudolf Hess, who would later become a high-ranking member of Hitler's inner circle. Hess acted as Hitler's secretary during their nine months behind bars, writing quickly as a Hitler spoke aloud his thoughts about his life and political philosophy. The result was volume one of *Mein Kampf* (*My Struggle*), published in 1925. At the time, people didn't pay much attention to Hitler's thoughts.

HITLER'S RISE

But ten years later, by the time he was appointed Germany's chancellor, they were paying a great deal of attention. During the intervening decade, Hitler had gathered power by his own determined actions and by the indecision of others. German politics featured a variety of rivals on both the right and left of the political spectrum. Some members of the right wing, notably former chancellor Franz von Papen, agreed to help Hitler. The left wing opposed Hitler and his Nazis to the end, but the most powerful parties on the left, the Social Democrats and the Communists, could never decide on a common strategy to block his rise to power.

Meanwhile, Hitler and his National Socialist German Workers Party (*Nationalsozialistische Deutsche Arbeiterpartie*), or Nazi Party for short, were becoming known around the world. A full-page illustration of Hitler glaring and shaking his fists appeared on the December 1931 cover of *Time* magazine. By 1932, the Nazi Party held 37 percent of the seats in the Reichstag, the German parliament, more than any other party. With the influence of von Papen, right-wing President Paul von Hindenburg was persuaded to appoint Hitler chancellor, the second most powerful government position.

Hitler took office on January 30, 1933. Having legally risen to second-in-command, Hitler quickly hatched a subversive and violent plot to grab more power. Twenty-four hours after his appointment, he persuaded von Hindenburg to dissolve the parliament and schedule new elections. The vote would take place on March 5.

CONSPIRACY

A key part of Hitler's conspiracy for power was his private police force. Chancellor Hitler quickly fired the police officials who were loyal to the existing German government and replaced them with loyal Nazi officials. He also installed his own private army and police forces: the

SA, also known as the brownshirts, and the SS, or storm troopers. Included in the SS was the Gestapo, Hitler's elite secret police force.

Hitler gave his forces unrestricted power. SA and SS officers were free to harass, beat, or even murder anyone they saw as disloyal to Hitler, especially members of the rival Communist Party.

Hitler also drew up the "Law for Removing the Distress of the People and the Reich," also known as the Enabling Act. If the German parliament voted yes on the act, it would mean the end of the Weimar Republic and the beginning of Nazi dictatorship.

This so-called "distress" actually came from Hitler's Nazi forces themselves. They had secretly burned the building housing the German government, the Reichstag, on February 27. Hitler claimed the fire was part of a widespread communist uprising that threatened the entire nation, and communist leaders were rounded up.

With their leaders in jail, the Communists lost votes in the May 5 elections. This helped the Nazis and their coalition ally, the German National People's Party, to come away with a 52 percent majority in the Reichstag.

MORE PRESSURE

Then came the Enabling Act vote on March 23, 1933. On the day of the vote, Hitler's storm troopers surrounded the building where the vote would take place. They were inside too, striking menacing poses and snarling out threats. If Hitler's proposals were voted down, they warned, more fires and other acts of sabotage were sure to follow.

Hitler tried portraying himself as conservative and thoughtful. In a speech to parliament, he promised that when lawmakers passed his act, he would use the new powers it gave him with careful restraint. But when a rival politician declared his opposition, Hitler flew into a rage, shouting, "The star of Germany will rise and yours will sink! Your death knell has sounded!"

Hitler's tactics worked. His Enabling Act passed by the needed two-thirds majority. Communist Party members were arrested. Other political parties either withdrew their opposition or were dissolved.

When President von Hindenburg died, in 1934, the role and powers of head of state were transferred to Hitler, who was now supreme commander of the military. The German electorate voted in favor of Hitler assuming supreme rule, making him dictator for life. Germany's experiment with democracy was out. Fascism was in.

Dressed to Terrorize

Every good dictator knows the value of terror as a tool for making sure his subjects toe the line. Hitler was a master at inspiring terror. His storm troopers were his primary instruments, and Hitler knew that where terror is involved, looks count.

So he had his storm troopers dress for maximum effect, like the official force of terror that they were. Fashion designer Hugo Boss designed the uniforms. They were either black or gray with the dreaded skeleton's head or *Totenkopf* on the cap visor, and the infamous double rune insignia that looked like twin lightning bolts on the collar tabs.

The uniform design was practical as well. During World War II, many SS men fought in the Panzer tank corps. Black was the right color for working around a lot of grease and oil. And the sleek wraparound tunic was designed without any buttons or flaps that might catch on a tank's small, tight hatch opening.

HITLER'S RACIAL HIERARCHY

In her classic book, *The Origins of Totalitarianism*, Hannah Arendt wrote that racism was the only ideology that "consistently denied the great principle upon which national organizations of people are built, the principle of equality and solidarity of all peoples guaranteed by the idea of mankind." Today, people tend to regard racial profiling as misinformed and morally wrong. But in Germany during Hitler's rise to power, it was a widely accepted way of looking at humankind, thanks in large part to eugenics.

In *Mein Kampf*, Hitler added a new element to the list of characteristics that supposedly separated the strong from the weak and the fit from the unfit: race. Hitler divided human beings into categories based on how they looked and on the ethnicity of their ancestors. Bloodlines and the color of skin, hair, and eyes meant far more than behavior and intelligence. According to Hitler, race was the one sure sign of a person's standing as a human being.

At the top of his racial rankings were the people Hitler labeled Aryans. These were the so-called *Ubermenschen*, the Germanic people with fair skin, blond hair, and blue eyes. This was Hitler's "master race."

Being born anything else made you an *Untermenschen*, a racially inferior person. The Untermenschen included the Jews and the Slavic peoples—the Poles, Czechs, and Russians, among others.

Adolf Hitler was the ultimate white supremacist. To him, the consequences of these racial divisions were simple and inevitable. History had destined the master race to rule all others.

HITLER'S GRAND PLAN

While Hitler despised capitalists and communists, he saw these non-Aryans, especially people of Jewish descent, as the real danger. His grand plan for the new German empire hinged on one simple, sweeping belief: The biological races of the world were fighting one another for survival. The Jews, the Slavs, and all the other "impure" races were battling the "pure" Aryans. The impure threatened to conquer the Aryans by breeding with them, thus contaminating their purity.

How could this threat be stopped? The only possible answer was all-out world war. Nation by nation, the Nazis would sweep across Europe and then the rest of the world. As the German army invaded

Adolf Hitler rose to power by claiming that Aryans were superior to other races. He enlisted children in his vision of a world run by the blue-eyed and blond. Here he stands with a member of the Nazi Youth group.

and conquered other nations, a vast empire would be built, a Third Reich. From those conquered nations the Nazis would rescue the Aryans and welcome them into this new German empire where they belonged.

What about the impure people? The Germans must "achieve the inner calm and outward strength brutally and ruthlessly to prune off the wild shoots and tear out the weeds," he wrote. In the end, Hitler predicted, an ideal world would arise, a utopia in which the righteous lived ideal lives while the unrighteous were left behind, imprisoned or dead.

To Adolf Hitler, history was no random series of events. It was not a story that made itself up as time ticked along. History was a tale already written out in full long, long ago. Now the long-completed tale was unfolding before our eyes, like a play or movie, with only one possible ending: the victory to which Hitler would lead the Aryan people, the planet's master race.

5
Mind Control

TOTALITARIAN DICTATORS AIM TO TRANSFORM their citizens' thoughts and opinions and reshape expectations. To achieve these goals, the dictator must first control the flow of information going out to the public. The mass communications technology of the twentieth century made it possible for a dictator such as Adolf Hitler to do this.

First the dictator seizes control of the mass media: the newspapers and magazines and radio and television stations that reach out to citizens all across the nation. There was no television in Hitler's time, but there was radio, a powerful medium to broadcast his captivating and emotional speeches.

Then the dictator decides what the media may publish and broadcast—and what they may not. Any information that people are allowed to take in must confirm his grand plan.

REALITY REDEFINED

For most people, the real world is something they must cope with on a daily basis. For a totalitarian dictator, the real world is a threat to his power. He rejects life as it's lived and people as they are and substitutes a fictitious world in which events happen and people think and behave according to a new set of rules.

This fictitious world does not square with the real world as people outside the dictatorship know it. But it does have the comforting virtue of consistency. The world that most people know is not neatly organized and predictable. Their plans seldom work out exactly as imagined; disruptive forces beyond human control contradict them.

But in a totalitarian world contradictions are strictly forbidden and everything, even history itself, is under firm control. This comforting illusion of a reality that unfolds strictly according to plan is one of the great appeals of dictatorship. In a 1936 speech, three years after Hitler took power, Nazi official Robert Ley described the rosy new world of the Third Reich according to Hitler:

> Germany has been born anew. The Führer said at the last Party rally, as he always says, that for him the greatest miracle of the age is how people have changed. Once there was hopelessness, today there is joy and affirmation, once there was general desperation, today there is resurrection and reawakening. Once each was the enemy of his neighbor. Envy, mistrust, and hatred were everywhere; today, everyone tries to do something good for the next person, even if sometimes with too much energy and enthusiasm. Each wants to be a good comrade, loyal, friendly.

PERSUASIVE PROPAGANDA

Most authoritarian dictators resort to terror to keep themselves in power and their people in line. Often their message can be boiled down to this: Do as I say or else.

But a totalitarian dictator must also persuade and convince his people that his fictitious world is, in fact, the real world, and that the nation is on the road to victory over all enemies. To persuade and convince, he resorts to propaganda.

This method of communicating with the public to advance national objectives comes in many forms. They include marches, parades, rallies, statues, motion pictures, paintings, textbooks, poems, photographs, magazine articles, billboards, murals, posters, signs—and speeches, such as Ley's.

Propaganda exists in societies run by other types of governments as well. In democracies much of it comes in the form of political and consumer product advertising. But in a democracy, no one is forced or even expected to be persuaded by all the propaganda they are exposed to each day. Otherwise they would have to vote for every candidate and buy every product. In a democracy, propaganda messages constantly compete with one another and people are free to choose which, if any, to believe. In a totalitarian dictatorship there are no competing points of view to choose from. You are expected to believe everything you are told, including news reports, as long as they come filtered through the state-run media.

NAZI CENSORS

No totalitarian dictator has used propaganda more inventively and effectively than Hitler. A key member of his inner circle was named Joseph Goebbels, Minister of Propaganda and National Enlightenment. Goebbels attended to two crucial tasks, each aimed at a single goal.

One task was making sure that no one in Germany heard or saw any information that was damaging to Naziism. His other task was making sure that the Nazi worldview was delivered to the people in the most persuasive form possible. If the German people could read, see, and hear only what Hitler wanted them to read, see, and hear, eventually they would believe it.

In 1933 Goebbels set up the Reich Chamber of Commerce to review everything published, played, broadcast, shown, and exhibited in the nation. People whose work did not meet party standards could not have their work published or performed.

But what about all the books published before Hitler came to power? Goebbels urged loyal Nazis to raid libraries and seize any offending volumes. Then the Nazis staged public book burnings. Goebbels and Hitler loved public spectacles, the bigger and more dramatic the better. The Nazis would heap the seized books into massive piles and make bonfires of them at night for maximum dramatic effect.

Authors whose books were burned included thinkers and writers of world renown, such as Albert Einstein, Franz Kafka, and Bertolt Brecht. A young woman living in Germany during Hitler's reign, Elfrida Bruenning, recalls the results of this censorship: "All the authors that we had treasured—and of course still do treasure—were suddenly supposed to be valueless."

PUBLIC DEMONSTRATIONS

Hitler ruled in the days before television, when radio was the dominant medium. So Goebbels ordered the mass manufacture of the "People's

Receiver," a radio cheap enough that anyone could afford it. Now all citizens could hear Hitler's speeches live in their homes.

If people were out in public, they could hear their dictator speaking to them through loudspeakers set up in the streets. Also, cafes and other public establishments were ordered to play Hitler's radio speeches for their customers.

Goebbels went so far as to have arenas built to hold 400,000 people, surround them with searchlights aimed skyward, and stage spectacular nighttime rallies, with Hitler himself as the main attraction. One of these rallies was held in 1934 in the city of Nuremberg, with more than one million Germans attending. The Nuremberg rally became the subject of a documentary film, *Triumph of the Will*. Some film critics still consider it the most powerful propaganda film of all time.

Triumph begins by showing a plane flying Hitler to the rally appearing out of thick, fluffy clouds and descending slowly and grandly to Earth, as if from Heaven. The rest of the film follows this theme of portraying Hitler as a living god. In his speech at the rally's closing ceremony, Hitler says that the Nazi Party "will be unchangeable in its doctrine, hard as steel in its organization, supple and adaptable in its tactics. In its entity, however, it will be like a religious order . . ."

Journalist William Shirer attended the Nuremberg rally. A few evenings before the event, he found himself in the midst of a crowd of thousands outside Hitler's hotel. Shirer wrote: "I was a little shocked at the faces when Hitler finally appeared on the balcony for a moment. . . . [T]hey looked up at him as if he were a Messiah, their faces transformed into something positively inhuman."

Adolf Hitler once said, "The masses are like an animal that obeys its instincts. They do not reach conclusions by reasoning. . . . At a mass meeting, thought is eliminated."

At the rally's opening event, Shirer saw the effects of Nazi propaganda first-hand:

> I am beginning to understand some of the reasons for Hitler's astounding success. Borrowing a chapter from the Roman [Catholic] church, he is restoring pageantry and color and mysticism to the drab lives of 20th Century Germans. This morning's opening meeting . . . was more than a gorgeous show, it also had something of the mysticism and religious fervor of an Easter or

Christmas Mass in a great Gothic cathedral. The hall was a sea of brightly colored flags. Even Hitler's arrival was made dramatic. The band stopped playing. There was a hush over the thirty thousand people packed in the hall. Then the band struck up the *Badenweiler March.* . . . Hitler appeared in the back of the auditorium and followed by his aides, Göering, Goebbels, Hess, Himmler and the others, he slowly strode down the long center aisle while thirty thousand hands were raised in salute.

Shirer summed up the effect this rally had on Hitler's audience by writing that "every word dropped by Hitler seemed like an inspired word from on high. Man's—or at least the German's—critical faculty is swept away at such moments, and every lie pronounced is accepted as high truth itself."

EXTREME PRIDE

Do totalitarian dictators believe all the propaganda about what great men they are? *Hubris* is another word that comes to mind when dictators like Hitler are mentioned. Hubris is a serious character flaw, an exaggerated pride or arrogance that often leads to tragedy.

Some dictators have gone so far as to proclaim themselves infallible and all-knowing. Benito Mussolini (1883–1945) was the fascist dictator of Italy, whose forces fought on Hitler's side in World War II. Mussolini would have crowds of schoolchildren brought to him and gathered close around just so he could stand and listen to them recite: "Mussolini is always right."

Few dictators could match Hitler for hubris. "As the ultimate factor I must, in all modesty, name my own person: irreplaceable. . . . The destiny of the Reich depends on me alone," he once said. And, "This is the miracle of our times . . . that you have found me among so many millions. And I have found you. That is Germany's fortune."

Hitler surrounded himself with men who would cater to this hubris. No one fawned over him more than Rudolf Hess. The following words are from one of Hess's speeches about his beloved leader:

With pride we see that one man remains beyond all criticism, that is the Führer. This is because everyone feels and knows:

he is always right, and he will always be right. The National Socialism of all of us is anchored in uncritical loyalty, in the surrender to the Führer that does not ask for the why in individual cases, in the silent execution of his orders. We believe that the Führer is obeying a higher call to fashion German history. There can be no criticism of this belief.

Hitler's extreme self-regard did not favorably impress everyone. Martha Dodd's father was the American ambassador to Germany during Hitler's reign, which gave her an opportunity to see Hitler in person. She described him as "insolent and arrogant, with shoulders flung back pompously, who walks and marches as though he had made the earth under his feet."

THE DICTATOR AND THE TRAMP

In fact, Hitler and his Nazis' extremes of mannerism and behavior, such as their goose-stepping marching style in which soldiers step forward without bending their knees, made them prime targets for satire. No one did a more effective job of ridiculing the Nazis than the British-American movie star and director Charlie Chaplin.

The Tramp, Chaplin's classic comic character, had appeared in dozens of short and feature films during the age of silent movies. The Tramp often poked fun at the other characters in the movie who were overbearing and self-important. Purely by coincidence, the Tramp's quirky little brush mustache strongly resembled Hitler's, as did Chaplin's height, weight, and facial structure. For Chaplin to satirize Hitler and his pompous Nazis on screen was too tempting to pass up.

Chaplin wrote, directed, and starred in *The Great Dictator*, a feature-length parody of Hitler and the Nazis. In 1940, when it was released, World War II was raging, with Hitler's Nazi armies invading European nations. The United States had not yet joined the war, but news reports had made Americans aware that Hitler posed a very real threat to civilization as they knew it.

The movie was widely hailed for its fearless condemnation and broad satire of the dictator and his Nazis. Chaplin plays Adenoid Hynkel, the Hitler-like leader. Nazi Germany is called Tomania, as in ptomaine poisoning. Fascist Italy, Germany's European partner in the war, is called Bacteria. The Nazis' dreaded insignia, the swastika,

"We Don't Want to Hate"

At the end of *The Great Dictator*, a Jewish barber who is mistaken for the title character must give a victory speech dressed in the dictator's uniform. Charlie Chaplin plays both roles. As the barber, he uses the opportunity to speak against everything the dictator stands for. Here is some of that eloquent speech:

> I'm sorry, but I don't want to be an emperor. That's not my business. I don't want to rule or conquer anyone. I should like to help everyone—if possible—Jew, Gentile, black man, white. We all want to help one another. Human beings are like that. We want to live by each other's happiness—not by each other's misery. We don't want to hate and despise one another. In this world there is room for everyone. And the good earth is rich and can provide for everyone. The way of life can be free and beautiful, but we have lost the way. Greed has poisoned men's souls, has barricaded the world with hate, has goose-stepped us into misery and bloodshed. We have developed speed, but we have shut ourselves in. Machinery that gives abundance has left us in want. Our knowledge has made us cynical. Our cleverness, hard and unkind. We think too much and feel too little. More than machinery we need humanity. More than cleverness we need kindness and gentleness. Without these qualities, life will be violent and all will be lost. . . .

became "the sign of the double cross." Hitler's propaganda minister, Goebbels, is called Gorbitsch (pronounced "Garbage").

The Great Dictator was a successful piece of anti-Nazi propaganda. It was also an enduring humanitarian film. Chaplin's call for the light of tolerance and love to shine in a world darkened by murderous intolerance and hatred served as a stirring indictment of Hitler's grand plan to kill millions in order to remake humanity.

6
Freedom and the Big Lie

Freedom is a dire threat to dictatorships. With it comes all sorts of possibilities, including thoughtfulness, which can lead to discontent, opposition, even revolution. In the fourth century BCE, Lord Shang, an advisor to Chinese rulers, wrote:

> The way to organize a country well is . . . to have no license [freedom] of speech. This being so the people will be simple and have concentration. . . . The way to administer a country well is for the law for the officials to be clear; therefore one does not rely on intelligent and thoughtful men. The ruler makes the people single-minded and therefore they will not scheme for selfish profit. Then the strength of the country will be consolidated. A country where the strength has been consolidated is powerful, but a country that loves talking is dismembered.

When he says that the law must be "clear," Lord Shang means simple, blunt, and uncomplicated. That's why he advises the ruler not to rely on "intelligent and thoughtful" advisors, who might not always see things in such a single-minded way. Debate and dissent are not welcome in a dictatorship.

MEETING THE THREAT

Totalitarian dictators aim to wipe out freedom. No one is at liberty to be "intelligent and thoughtful" if it leads to questioning authority. In a dictatorship, the basic civil liberties that a democracy guarantees, including speech, assembly, and religion, must be suspended.

When Hitler grabbed dictatorial power in 1933, he gained the right to pass laws that restricted constitutional rights, such as freedom of the press, rights of assembly, and free expression of opinion. These laws were stated in language so broad that authorities could arrest almost anyone for saying or doing almost anything. Even the most minor offense could get a person a long jail sentence or even the death penalty.

Basic rights of privacy were curbed as well. People's postal, telegraphic, and telephone communications could be monitored by the government. Restrictions on searches and seizures of private property also were suspended. Anything people did, said, or possessed was not truly theirs anymore. It all belonged to the state.

EUGENICS AND FREEDOM

In order to create the perfect human beings who would build the perfect society, Hitler promoted eugenics with great enthusiasm. This meant that some people would have to give up their freedom to choose whom they would marry.

In 1934 the Nazis passed the Law for the Prevention of Offspring with Hereditary Diseases, which called for a racial screening of the entire German population to determine who could marry whom and who should be sterilized. By law, Germans could not marry Jews, and healthy people could not marry those with a disability or a hereditary illness.

Healthy partners were encouraged to have as many children as possible. Aryan women who qualified as "good breeders" were rewarded. During World War II, with many German soldiers being killed in combat, Aryan widows received even greater rewards for producing more Aryan children out of wedlock.

THE MASS MAN

Hitler's perfect human beings had to be psychologically as well as physically superior. Their personalities had to be taken apart and put back together so that they no longer behaved like unique individuals. This new kind of person became known as the mass man.

Adolf Hitler's "vision" was of the creation of a mass of men who moved, looked, and acted as one. This poster shows the look of the man Hitler believed he had created.

To transform an ordinary person into a mass man, all social and family ties, religious ties, and cultural ties had to be cut. The mass man could feel no loyalty toward any group or individual outside the state. Once the people were isolated from one another and emptied of all normal human ties and loyalties, they were completely dependent on their government and ready to be formed into units to serve the state.

Did the Nazis really succeed in creating the mass man? Here is Hitler's opinion. As he marveled at the sight of sixty thousand members of his secret police assembled for his inspection, he said that these men "have outwardly become almost a unit, that actually these members are uniform not only in ideas, but that even the facial expression is almost the same. Look at these laughing eyes, this fanatical enthusiasm and you will discover . . . how a hundred thousand men in a movement become a single type."

INVENTING ENEMIES

As much as a totalitarian dictator needs obedient subjects, he also needs hated enemies. Sometimes they live outside the dictator's nation, like the citizens of the Allied Powers who inflicted such an unexpected and humiliating defeat on Germany in World War I.

More often they live within the nation's borders. Every dictator has political opponents, even if they operate only in secret. But a totalitarian dictator sees his political opponents as more than mere rivals. He sees them as traitors: a dire threat to the success of his grand plan.

Often these so-called enemies are not political opponents. In fact they pose no real threat at all. The dictator only says they do. He tends to pick on people who are perfectly harmless. How does he go about turning innocent people into enemies of the state?

First he dehumanizes and demonizes them. Hitler called the Jewish people "beasts, criminals, conspirators, traitors, well-poisoners," among other hateful epithets. A Nazi propaganda pamphlet from 1941 insisted that the Jews were plotting "the complete sterilization of the German people" and "the complete extermination of Germandom and its bearers." The pamphlet also insisted that the U.S. president at the time, Franklin D. Roosevelt, was part of this "murderous program."

No such plan, plot, or murderous program existed. In fact, the opposite was true. Hitler used the Jews as scapegoats, blaming them for crimes they had nothing to do with. Hitler and the Nazis were the ones plotting the crimes. They planned on exterminating the Jewish people.

The Big Lie

Like other dictators, Adolf Hitler knew a thing or two about lying to the public. Here in this passage from *Mein Kampf* are his thoughts on how to succeed in the art of lying by lying big.

> [I]n the big lie there is always a certain force of credibility; because the broad masses of a nation are always more easily corrupted in the deeper strata of their emotional nature than consciously or voluntarily; and thus in the primitive simplicity of their minds they more readily fall victims to the big lie than the small lie, since they themselves often tell small lies in little matters but would be ashamed to resort to large-scale falsehoods. It would never come into their heads to fabricate colossal untruths, and they would not believe that others could have the impudence to distort the truth so infamously. Even though the facts which prove this to be so may be brought clearly to their minds, they will still doubt and waver and will continue to think that there may be some other explanation. For the grossly impudent lie always leaves traces behind it, even after it has been nailed down, a fact which is known to all expert liars in this world and to all who conspire together in the art of lying. These people know only too well how to use falsehood for the basest purposes.

Hitler declared that the Nazis needed to "bloodily, swiftly destroy and shoot [the Jews], burn out these ulcers of the raw flesh, grasp them ruthlessly and bloodily."

CRIMINALS WITHOUT A CRIME

Hitler knew he was unlikely to succeed in rallying millions of ordinary Germans to murder millions of perfectly innocent souls in cold blood. Not even the mass man could be expected to kill people he had no reason to fear or dislike. So Hitler and the Nazis used a propaganda technique known as "the big lie" to portray the Jews as treacherous, relentless, deadly aggressors who threatened the Aryan people with racial extermination.

The stereotyped image that many Germans already had of Jewish people fit their role of scapegoat perfectly. First, the Jews had no nation of their own. The independent nation of Israel wasn't created until 1948, after Hitler had murdered six million Jews. So the Nazis could convincingly portray the Jews as outsiders, foreigners, parasites who used the German people's nation to make themselves a comfortable home.

The Jews were also seen as members of the upper class but not the governing class. According to this view, instead of helping to run the country, they kept a low profile, trying not to call attention to themselves as they lived their wealthy lives for their own selfish benefit.

This supposed secretiveness fit right into the role of plotters and schemers that Nazi propaganda used to portray this supposed Jewish enemy. They were lying in wait, all set to destroy the Aryan nation. And stereotyping Jews as wealthy stirred up envy on the part of all the German citizens suffering through tough financial times.

All this outrageous anti-Jewish stereotyping and propaganda was patently untrue. German Jews lived just like the rest of the population, only with fewer rights. Not everyone bought Hitler's lies. Throughout Europe there were charges of anti-Semitism, especially in the nations that the Nazis conquered.

Within Germany, though, this anti-Jewish propaganda campaign accomplished its goals. Hitler managed to create a convincing them-or-us, kill-or-be-killed scenario. Once he had the majority of the German people convinced that the Jews were a dire threat, the stage was set. Now Hitler could rally the people to heroically defend themselves against this "deadly enemy."

7
The Holocaust and Defeat

THE NAZIS KEPT PERSONAL FILES on their citizens. During World War II (1939–1945), they put together the German Racial Register, which contained the photographs and medical records of some 1.5 million men and women throughout Europe.

From these records, they separated out the individuals they considered true Aryans, who would be welcomed into Hitler's empire. The others ended up on the enemies list. These "impure" people were destined to be exiled, imprisoned, sterilized, or executed.

THE UNDESIRABLES

Many types of people were on the Nazis' enemies list. They included Roma (or Gypsies), habitual criminals, sex offenders, people known to have had sex outside of marriage, homosexuals, and people with physical and mental disabilities. Eventually some 360,000 were sterilized in the name of racial purity.

Ordinary citizens were strongly encouraged to help the police identify undesirables by telling the authorities of any suspicious activities. Knowing they stood a better chance of escaping arrest if they cast suspicion on others, some people turned in their friends and neighbors.

Hitler's 45,000-man Gestapo force had the uncontested right to take into protective custody anyone the Nazis felt presented a potential danger to the state. This so-called protective custody usually led to either unlimited confinement or execution, without the right to a trial.

GERMAN CITIZENS PROTEST

The German people grew to accept much of this punishment as necessary or at least looked the other way, but sometimes the Nazis went to extremes the people couldn't accept. In 1939, Hitler secretly ordered the systematic killing of handicapped children throughout Germany. Two years later, when the public learned of the killing, there was so much outrage that the Nazis had to suspend the program.

Some German citizens did actively speak out and protest the killings the Nazis were carrying out both at home and on foreign battlefields. They were convinced that Hitler's Nazis were brutal and unjust and they wanted the war to end quickly with a German defeat.

But public outrage was rare and became rarer as the war moved on and the nation threw all its resources into fighting its foreign enemies: France, Great Britain, and the other Allied nations that the Nazis were attacking in their campaign to conquer the world. With this war of combat facing them, the German people were distracted from the Nazis' secret war against "impure" German citizens.

ROUNDING UP VICTIMS

The Nazis' "Final Solution of the Jewish Question," as they called it, was clear and simple. It was genocide: to exterminate all Jews from the face of the earth, step by step.

Hitler's first step was to isolate Jews from the general population. The German Racial Register helped the Nazis locate Jews in Germany and, later, in the other European nations that Nazi armies invaded and occupied. First on the list was Czechoslovakia in 1938. By 1940 the Nazis had added Poland, Norway, Denmark, France, Belgium, Luxembourg, and Holland.

The Jews in every country were rounded up and put into ghettos. A ghetto is a part of a city, sometimes sealed off, where people of a common ethnic background are forced to live segregated from the rest of society. Altogether, between 1939 and 1945, the Nazis set up 356 ghettos to hold European Jews. The first Jewish ghettos were established in large cities in Poland. The largest of these, the Warsaw ghetto, held 380,000 people.

THE GHETTOS

European Jews had lived in ghettos before, but this was the first time in history that ghettos had been used as holding areas for people facing imprisonment, starvation, and execution. To hide this brutal fact, Hitler had a model ghetto built in Czechoslovakia. It was called Terezin, or in German, Theresienstadt. Terezin had schools, cafes, and flower gardens.

The International Red Cross was a humanitarian organization that sent representatives out to inspect prisoner of war camps. They also wanted to inspect one of the ghettos, so inspectors were invited to witness the humane conditions at Terezin, a "typical" Jewish ghetto.

By referring to them as "Jewish residential districts," the Nazis tried to make the ghettos sound respectable and homey. They were anything but. Typical ghettos were nothing like Terezin. They were filthy. Sanitation was poor. Housing was sparse and overcrowded. Disease spread like wildfire. Lack of warm clothing and fuel for heating made winters harrowing tests of survival for the residents. And with food in such short supply, many people starved to death. Most ghettos were surrounded by brick walls, wooden fences, or barbed wire. Guards were placed at all openings, and Jews who tried to escape faced the penalty of death.

WITHDRAWING RIGHTS

The way the rest of the world reacted to the situation gave the Nazis confidence. No country offered to take in the millions of Jews they were rounding up and confining to ghettos. With no nation of their own and no nation to claim them, the Jews of Europe made ideal victims.

But Hitler did not want the outside world to witness the cold-blooded execution of millions of defenseless souls. Before he could take the final step of exterminating Europe's Jews, he had to remove them and hide them away.

Hitler did this methodically. First came the denial of basic rights. Starting in 1939, German Jews were forbidden to work as dentists, veterinarians, or chemists. In 1940, the German people were forbidden to employ Jewish women in their homes. In 1941, after the Nazis invaded and occupied Poland, Polish Jews were prohibited from using public transportation.

As the Nazis occupied other European nations, they curbed the

Resistance

Germany and the Soviet Union were allies for a short while at the start of World War II and fought the rest of the war as enemies. In 1944, the Soviet army drove the Nazis out of the Eastern European city of Kovno, Lithuania, where a Jewish ghetto built by the Nazis lay in ruins. Like many Jews in ghettos throughout Europe, the occupants of Kovno had resisted the Nazis, getting hold of weapons, escaping, and mounting attacks against their captors.

In retaliation, the Nazis had blown up and burned down the Kovno ghetto before fleeing from the oncoming Soviets. All but a handful of Kovno's Jewish resisters were killed. Looking through the ruins, a Soviet soldier found a book containing notes written by his brother, who had died in the ghetto. Here is some of what the Soviet soldier read.

> People! We are locked up like animals here. For seven days we had been hiding from our executioners in the loft without water, in terrible heat. Then we were attacked with grenades and our house was set on fire. We managed to escape into the cellar. A great number of people in the house have already perished. . . . Comrades! Revenge us! There used to be about forty thousand Jews in Kovno. We are only few remaining . . . People! Annihilate the Fascist scum. No mercy! . . . Let . . . mankind rid [itself] of the worst evil in its history. Comrades! May the sacred revenge become the essence of your life!

rights of Jews there as well. Jews in France were forbidden to enter cafes. In occupied Holland, the Nazis banned Jewish music. Meanwhile, more and more European Jews were being rounded up and confined to ghettos.

Being identified as a Jew and put into a ghetto meant that you were now without rights. You could no longer call yourself a genuine citizen of your nation, and you no longer enjoyed protection by the law. You were treated like the refugee of a conquered nation or a prisoner of war. You had no one to turn to and nowhere to go. Now you were prepared for your final destination.

DEPORTATION

One more step remained in the genocide of the European Jews. The ghettos were still attached to cities. Even if the Jews themselves were hidden from view, people still could see where they were confined. Hitler needed the Jews out of sight entirely—and out of mind, he hoped. That is why, in 1942, the Nazis began deporting Jews to concentration camps.

The first camps were set up in Germany, starting in 1933. In the beginning they were designed to hold all the many kinds of people whom the Nazis judged unfit to live. During the war, many more camps had to be built to hold and kill prisoners of war and all the Jews from the conquered nations. Camps were built in Poland, Czechoslovakia, the Soviet Union, Norway, Lithuania, and France. By the war's end, some 15,000 Nazi concentration camps had been constructed.

Most of the inmates were Jews brought from the ghettos by rail. They were loaded into freight cars and crowded so close together that many died before reaching their destination.

Upon arrival, the survivors were quickly shown just how truly alone in the world and helpless they were. Here is Holocaust survivor Leo Schneiderman's description of his arrival at the camp in Auschwitz, Germany:

> It was late at night that we arrived at Auschwitz. When we came in, the minute the gates opened up, we heard screams, barking of dogs. . . . And then we got out of the train. And everything went so fast: left, right, right, left. Men separated from women. Children torn from the arms of mothers. The elderly chased like cattle. The sick, the

disabled were handled like packs of garbage. They were thrown . . . together with broken suitcases, with boxes. My mother ran over to me and grabbed me by the shoulders, and she told me "Leibele, I'm not going to see you no more. Take care of your brother."

THE FINAL SOLUTION: GENOCIDE

This was only the first in a series of events designed to break down each inmate's will and prepare them all for death. The concentration camps were also called death camps, with good reason. Six million Jews and five million others would die there. Some would starve to death. Others would be worked to death. Most would be executed in gas chambers, and their bodies cremated or buried in mass graves.

This systematic persecution and genocide of the Jews in Europe became known as the Holocaust. The word comes from Greek words meaning "complete destruction."

Jews were not the only group targeted in the Holocaust. When other targeted groups, such as homosexuals, Roma, and the mentally ill are added in, most estimates set the number at about 11 million.

The Nazis' special term for the Holocaust, the "Final Solution to the Jewish Question," reflected their cold-blooded, methodical approach to the business of doing away with millions of innocent people. In the fictitious world in which Hitler and his Nazis lived, they were doing nothing in the least bit inhumane or immoral. Their aim was simply to solve this "problem" as efficiently and economically as possible.

Most of the children under the age of twelve were taken immediately to the gas chambers, since they were too young to work. The Nazis used most of the other prisoners for slave labor—used them until they died from disease or starved to death. In this way even these enemies/ victims played their part in Hitler's grand plan.

IDEAL VERSUS REAL

Journalist Bill Moyers wrote, "[I]deologies hold stoutly to a world view despite being contradicted by what is generally accepted as reality." These words apply all too well to totalitarian dictators, who design an ideal world run by a set of rules very different from the rules by which the real world runs. Their grand plans are met with resistance and rebellion, economic catastrophe, famine, and defeats on the battlefield: one setback after another.

The Nazis were responsible for the murder of more than six million Jews and about five million others who did not fit their description of the "master race." At the German concentration camp of Belsen, piles of boots of the dead were used for fuel by its prisoners.

But these leaders remain resolute, staying the course no matter what, refusing to face the painful truth. Historian Richard Overy calls it "the myth of perfectibility." He writes: "Utopias do not and cannot exist. They are by their nature ideal but unobtainable . . ." Instead, they produce the very opposite, a dystopia: "a nightmare of violence, discrimination, persecution and misrepresentation."

A dictator may possess absolute political power, but he still must contend with the real world and forces beyond his control. Eventually the disappointing truth comes out. For Hitler, it was the fact that his Aryan race was not the master race after all.

HITLER'S DOWNFALL

As early as June of 1941, two years into the war, Nazi leaders were starting to see the cracks in the Aryan armor. Joseph Goebbels, Hitler's Minister of Propaganda, wrote in his diary:

> The *Fuhrer* says: right or wrong, we must win. It is the only way. And victory is right, moral and necessary. And once we have won, who is going to question our methods? In any case, we have so much to answer for already that we must win, because otherwise our entire nation—with us at its head—and all we hold dear will be eradicated.

The United States joined the war against Germany, Italy, and Japan in December 1941, following the Japanese attack on the U.S. Navy fleet in Pearl Harbor, Hawaii. The Nazis continued their march across Europe, but with most of the rest of the world against them, their momentum faltered. Britain and the Soviet Union could not be conquered. By the spring of 1945 the war was all but over. The German army had collapsed, and Hitler had retreated into a bunker in Germany's capital, Berlin.

Looking back on those days, Hitler's secretary, Erna Flegal, said, "In the last few days Hitler sank into himself." Then, on April 30, with the victorious Soviet army approaching, Hitler's life came to an end. Exactly what happened can't be known for certain, but this scenario seems most likely: Hitler shot himself in the right temple after his wife, Eva Braun, swallowed a fatal dose of cyanide. Members of Hitler's personal SS bodyguard carried the corpses out of the bunker into a nearby garden, doused them with gasoline, and burned them.

GERMANY AFTER HITLER

Looking back from the Germany of today to the Germany of 1945 shows a startling transformation. The ghost of Hitler still haunted the land of postwar Germany. Former storm troopers, acting as terrorists, committed sabotage and attacked both Allied occupation forces and German locals. They were rounded up as part of an Allied campaign to de-Nazify postwar Germany.

Meanwhile, the once powerful German economy lay in ruins, along with much of the nation itself, flattened by bombing raids and land campaigns. Rebuilding Germany would be a difficult process.

Although the Allies wanted the new Germany to remain a single state, it first split into two states in 1949, one independent and democratic and the other Communist, controlled by the Soviet Union. The nation was finally reunited in 1990. Today the Federal Republic of Germany is a founding member of the European Union (EU), a family of democratic European countries committed to working together for peace and prosperity. Germany is the EU's most economically powerful member.

8

Stalin's Grand Plan ■ ■ ■

TOTALITARIAN DICTATORSHIPS DO NOT TAKE root in wealthy nations run by strong and popular governments. For a dictator such as Hitler to rise to power, he must have a troubled nation to rule. Joseph Stalin, another totalitarian leader, came along at the same time in history as Hitler. From 1939–1941 they were allies in World War II, then fought bitterly against each another to the war's end, with the Soviets playing a key role in defeating the Nazis.

Their nations were very different in size. Hitler's Germany was dwarfed by the Soviet Union. Stalin's vast empire stretched from central Europe all the way to the Pacific Ocean and from the Arctic to the Afghanistan border. All in all, the Soviet Union covered one-sixth of Earth's land surface. Its people numbered nearly 150 million and represented more than a hundred different nationalities.

THE SOVIET REVOLUTION

These two nations were alike in another way. Like Germany, the Soviet Union was a nation in transition. It was a monarchy until 1917 when a revolution toppled the ruling monarch, Tsar Nicholas II.

The new provisional government was opposed by the Bolsheviks, a political movement led by Vladimir Lenin. Lenin inspired an armed revolution against this temporary government. "All power to the Soviets!" was his call to arms.

ЛЕНИН–
ЖИЛ,
ЛЕНИН–
ЖИВ,
ЛЕНИН–
БУДЕТ ЖИТЬ!

ВЛ. МАЯКОВСКИЙ.

Vladimir Ilyich Lenin led the Communist Revolution in Russia against the dictatorial regime. Ironically, Lenin and the communist leaders who followed would become dictators themselves.

With this revolution, the Bolsheviks successfully seized power and Lenin became the Soviet Union's virtual dictator. Lenin's dictatorial policies would pave the way for Stalin's rise more than a decade later.

In 1918 Lenin renamed the Bolsheviks the Communist Party. At this time Lenin and his new party officially subscribed to the twin ideologies of socialism and communism.

SOCIALISM AND COMMUNISM

Two books defined and inspired socialist and communist movements in Europe during Lenin's and Stalin's time. Karl Marx's *Das Kapital*, published in 1867, was a harsh critique of capitalism, the economic system of Western nations such as Great Britain and the United States. For the workers of the world, Marx claimed, capitalism posed an insidious dilemma, since the land and the means of production, distribution, and transport of goods were privately owned.

Private ownership, according to Marx, inevitably led the owners into exploiting the workers. The more the workers produced, the more the owners profited, and the more they profited the greedier they became, and this spiraling greed encouraged the owners to exploit the workers even more. The few kept profiting while the many kept losing. For the worker, the capitalist system was a no-win situation, according to Marx.

The answer to capitalism was socialism, Marx's revolutionary economic system. The workers had to free themselves from the bonds of capitalism through revolution, Marx wrote. They must overthrow the old state and create a new democratic state in which they, not the owners, controlled the means of production and shared equally in the benefits.

The other book, *The Communist Manifesto*, by Marx and Friedrich Engels, published in 1848, described the last stages of this socialist revolution, after capitalism had been overthrown. In this ideal communist society, people's attitude toward work had changed. They no longer worked because they had to, they worked because they wanted to, which inspired them to produce more. There was no wealthy ruling class anymore and no more poor. Material goods were produced in such abundance that everyone lived well. With society running so smoothly, the benign central government had no reason to interfere in people's lives, so everyone was both well-provided for and free to live as they pleased.

LENIN PAVES THE WAY

Lenin's policies were supposed to be based on Marx's writings. But as Marxism morphed into Marxism-Leninism, Marx's socialist and communist ideals became more and more unrecognizable. Instead of working toward a democratic nation, Lenin was busy creating his own brand of totalitarianism.

He wiped away civil liberties, including freedom of the press. He persecuted the intellectual class and religious leaders. Lenin established one-party rule, and when peasants, workers, and sailors revolted against it, he had those revolts crushed. He also purged some 260,000 people from the party, those he considered to be disloyal or a threat to his power. On the economic front, Lenin nationalized factories, mines, banks, and public utilities. Now the government owned the means of production, but the workers did not benefit.

Although his economic plans failed badly, Lenin still managed to lay the groundwork for the totalitarian society that the Soviet Union would become under Stalin. He accomplished all this in the space of just seven years in power, dying from a stroke in 1924.

STALIN'S RISE

Joseph Stalin was born in 1878. He spent his early adult years as a full-time revolutionary. His work included organizing workers to strike and demonstrate against factory owners. He kept at these provocative activities even though it meant years spent in exile as punishment.

Stalin joined the Bolshevik party in 1904 and rose through its ranks. Lenin needed a man who was a good bureaucratic organizer, self-reliant, and decisive, and Stalin met these needs. Lenin also demanded loyalty, and again Stalin filled the bill, never opposing Lenin's policies while Lenin was alive. Stalin worked hard and steadily and remained in the background until 1922, when he became general secretary of the party's Central Committee, a powerful position.

After Lenin's death in 1927, Stalin went to work consolidating his power. He plotted to make his party colleagues suspicious of each other and watched quietly as they eliminated one another. Meanwhile, Stalin was busy inserting his own loyal followers in positions to support him.

By 1928, Stalin controlled the party, and therefore all of Soviet politics. He was, for all practical purposes, absolute dictator of the Soviet Union. Leninism was out. Stalinism was in.

Precautionary Measures

Like many dictators, Stalin was keenly aware that assassins would be out to get him, and he took strict measures to protect himself. The automobiles of Stalin's day had running boards, narrow strips of footboard beneath the doors, which people used when entering and exiting. The running boards on Stalin's official cars were removed to keep assassins from jumping aboard, and the cars were thickly armored to deflect an assassin's bullets.

No place was safe. Would-be assassins might be lurking anywhere. Whenever Stalin was in a room that had curtains, they had to be trimmed at the bottom so that no one could hide behind them without their feet being seen.

Joseph Stalin became head of the Communist Party when Lenin died. During his regime (1928–1953) he industrialized the nation and imprisoned or killed millions whom he saw as enemies of the revolution.

REMAKING A NATION

Stalin quickly decreed that the Soviet Union would be industrialized and modernized. A poor nation of peasant farmers would be transformed into an industrial giant to rival the capitalist nations of the West. "We are fifty or a hundred years behind the advanced countries," Stalin said in 1929. "We must make good this distance in ten years. Either we do it, or we shall go under."

But Stalin's Soviet Union was largely an agricultural country. There were relatively few Soviet factories and little money available to build more. That money would have to come from the peasants, Stalin decreed.

Under Stalin, Soviet peasants were made to change radically the way they farmed. They had to give up their private land, join forces, and farm together in state-run communes supervised by Communist Party officials. Instead of using simple tools, groups of farm families were ordered to work large-scale plots of land using mechanized farm equipment.

In Stalin's mind this would enable them to produce more crops than ever before. This surplus food supply would go to feed the growing population of industrial workers in the new Soviet factories.

The peasants were also ordered to drastically scale down their already low standard of living. By receiving less for their work and consuming less, they would leave more capital for the building of factories.

UNREACHABLE GOALS

Stalin moved his revolution along in the form of five-year national economic plans. Each plan set goals for the amount of crops or industrial goods that the nation's workers must produce. Under these plans, Stalin predicted, both agricultural and industrial production would rise dramatically.

Stalin's plans proved to be crude and unrealistic. Workers were forever being pushed to produce more. Before they could meet one five-year plan's production quotas, Stalin would announce a new plan with even higher, more unreachable goals.

Like other dictators, Stalin had a habit of giving lip service to ideas he had no intention of practicing. This gigantic push to transform a backward nation into a modern state was supposed to propel the Soviet

Union toward becoming a truly Communist society, where the people produced an abundance of goods as a benign government looked approvingly on. Instead, his permanent agricultural and industrial revolution left the nation mired in perpetual impoverishment and instability.

Vanishing Freedoms 9 ▮ ▮ ▮

WHEN THE SUBJECT OF DICTATORS ARISES, the word *cult* often comes to mind: a group devoted to beliefs and aims that are different from those of most of society. At the center of the cult is the dictator himself, the one with all the power. He must supply the grand plan, the inspiration to work toward it, and the confidence that in time it will succeed.

That adds up to a heavy burden of responsibility for one person to bear, a lot of people depending upon him for a lot of different things. How does a dictator keep the people convinced that he can meet all these needs?

BIGGER THAN LIFE

He uses propaganda to develop what political scientists refer to as a "cult of personality." His goal is to elevate himself to such a godlike status that no one would even think of disobeying him.

To create this cult he commissions artists and writers to produce works that glorify him. Portraits that hang in homes and public places depict him in different kinds of clothing to show the many roles he plays. Massive statues show him in heroic positions. Books of his speeches and thoughts appear everywhere in bookstores, libraries, and classrooms.

Public spectacles to honor him play a key role. They give him an

Dictators use propaganda to maintain their hold on their people. North Koreans in military uniform perform near a display of heroic soldier images formed by thousands of children holding up cards during an annual massive propaganda spectacle known as a "mass game."

opportunity to present himself to the nation in awesome surroundings, often with soldiers and weapons on proud and intimidating display. Like Hitler, he may glory in this show of power, swelling his chest and strutting back and forth. Or he may present himself as modest and humble in the face of all this praise and admiration. That way the carefully staged display of public support and affection appears more spontaneous and genuine, and he appears as the kindly and just protector, the nation's father.

STALIN'S CULT OF PERSONALITY

No dictator is more famous for developing a cult of personality than Joseph Stalin. Soviet composer Dimitri Shostakovich knew Stalin personally. He described him as "an ordinary, shabby little man: short, fat, with reddish hair. His face was covered with pock marks and his right hand was noticeably thinner than his left. He kept hiding his right hand. He didn't look anything like his numerous portraits."

With the help of an ongoing propaganda campaign, Stalin managed to transform his image from a "shabby little man" to a virtual god. Vagif Samadoghlu is a poet and playwright from the former Soviet state of Azerbaijan, which is now an independent nation. The first time he saw Stalin in person was in 1951 at a New Year's Eve celebration in Moscow. Samadoghlu was twelve years old at the time. He remembers dancing a waltz with a girl from East Germany when Stalin entered the hall:

> Suddenly, somebody shouted: 'Stop, stop!' and the music stopped. Stalin walked into the hall wearing a white uniform. I was shocked when I saw him—he was so short. I had pictured him to be a large charismatic figure who could hardly fit through the door. After all, that's the way all his statues looked. . . .

> He waved at us and that was our signal to let our voices ring out in unison: "Long live Stalin!" One girl fainted from excitement.

Here is another remembrance that shows Stalin's personality cult in action. It comes from the daughter of a Soviet official, who saw Stalin in person at a 1936 gathering of political leaders:

I have never heard a public speaker so unhurried, so confident that not only every word of his was being listened to but also that he could make whatever pauses he liked and they would not seem empty. . . . [H]e was like a stage director, pausing at places where there should be laughter, and we would laugh . . . I clapped; everyone clapped. I was ecstatic, in a state of exaltation. And then there was the thrill of being in the presence of the tremendous power that could be felt all around.

What happens to the nation's citizens when their dictator is elevated to a godlike status? They may have gained a great deal, but what have they lost?

HYMN TO STALIN

This letter of praise to Stalin, written by Soviet author A. O. Avdienko in 1936, shows just how deeply attached the Russian people were to their leader. It also demonstrates how successful Stalin was in creating a cult of personality for himself.

Thank you, Stalin. Thank you because I am joyful. Thank you because I am well. No matter how old I become, I shall never forget how we received Stalin two days ago. Centuries will pass, and the generations still to come will regard us as the happiest of mortals, as the most fortunate of men, because we lived in the century of centuries, because we were privileged to see Stalin, our inspired leader. Yes, and we regard ourselves as the happiest of mortals because we are the contemporaries of a man who never had an equal in world history.

The men of all ages will call on thy name, which is strong, beautiful, wise and marvelous. Thy name is engraven on every factory, every machine, every place on the earth, and in the hearts of all men.

Every time I have found myself in his presence I have been subjugated by his strength, his charm, his grandeur. I have experienced a great desire to sing, to cry out, to shout with joy and happiness . . .

I write books. I am an author. All thanks to thee, O great educator, Stalin. I love a young woman with a renewed love and shall perpetuate myself in my children—all thanks to thee, great educator, Stalin. I shall be eternally happy and joyous, all thanks to thee, great educator, Stalin. Everything belongs to thee, chief of our great country. And when the woman I love presents me with a child the first word it shall utter will be: Stalin.

FREEDOM OF OPINION

Since the days of Lenin, the Soviet government had been on a campaign to deny people's basic freedoms. Stalin continued this tradition. In Stalin's Soviet Union, freedom of opinion had disappeared to make way for the world according to Joseph Stalin, known as the "general Party line."

On any subject there could be only one opinion, the one held by Stalin's Soviet Communist Party. People could no longer say what they thought without first asking themselves: Does this violate the general party line in some way? Anyone uttering words to the contrary risked punishment.

Naturally, most people wanted to conform their speech to the party line and avoid punishment. The problem was, the truth kept changing. For example, a historian was punished simply for saying that Joan of Arc was nervous and tense as she was about to be burned at the stake. He did not know that the official opinion on Joan of Arc had changed. At that moment in time, the party line said that she was calm in the face of death, not nervous.

Intellectuals like this unfortunate historian were especially likely to be singled out for punishment. Persecution of the intelligentsia had begun with Lenin, and Stalin carried on the tradition with enthusiasm. He was known for his suspicion and hatred of people he saw as more intelligent and of a higher cultural class than himself. This included anyone in the educated classes, from engineers to office workers to librarians. Many of these political prisoners were exiled to forced labor camps, or *gulags*, where inmates often were forced to work in inhumane contitions. While these camps contained criminals of all types, they became notorious as places of punishment for anyone seen as opposing Stalin's policies.

Lenin versus God

An incident in Baku, Azerbaijan, shows how determined the Communist Party was to "correct" people's attitude toward religion. The incident took place in a city park in 1918.

A group of schoolchildren were told that today their religious faith would be put to the test. They were directed to pray to God for their lunch. After a while, when no lunch had appeared, they were told to direct their request to Communist Party leader Lenin instead.

A few minutes later, trucks full of cheese, fruit, and bread drove up to the park. There, the children were told. Now they could see for themselves that it was Lenin who gave bread, not God.

FREEDOM OF RELIGION

Freedom of religion also was denied, but the nation had a long and deep religious tradition that many Soviets were not willing to give up. This persistent attitude presented a real problem for Stalin's Communist Party, which saw religion as a prime enemy of the state.

Karl Marx had written that religion led to an illusory happiness, arguing for a human spiritual essence that had no basis in reality. He called religion the opiate of the people, a kind of spiritual drug that dulled the pain of oppression and, by dulling it, kept people slaves to that oppression, denying them true happiness.

In order for people to escape from the oppression of the capitalist system, they could have no loyalties or guiding faith outside of the state. To bring this about, the Communist Party had churches shut down, clergymen deported or killed, religious property sold off, and religion banned in the schools. Despite this anti-religion campaign, a 1937 census revealed that 57 percent of the population still classified themselves as believers.

10
Terror and Decline

HITLER HAD HIS GESTAPO AND STORM TROOPERS. Stalin also had his private enforcers, the Communist secret police, known as the NKVD. In 1934, Stalin passed a law that gave them absolute power. The NKVD stood ready to deal with anyone the dictator saw as a threat to his power. Stalin was known for being intensely suspicious. He saw threats everywhere and was constantly targeting people for arrest.

It was understood that those Stalin targeted were automatically guilty. These supposed enemies were either plotting against him personally or attempting to overthrow the Communist government.

The NKVD would arrest these targets and interrogate them relentlessly until they confessed. This might take several days and nights. By then most prisoners were too exhausted and confused to resist anymore, and they would sign confessions whether or not they were guilty. The secret police could then execute these prisoners immediately.

PARANOIA AND PURGES

Stalin was also known for his ruthless manipulation of people for personal gain. No one was above suspicion, including members of his own Bolshevik Party. In fact, Stalin's party purges made it clear that the more loyalty someone showed, the less that person could be trusted. Throughout his reign Stalin kept changing the faces around him.

Purge has a special political meaning: the process of removing undesirable people from positions of power in a government or political party. It's a kind of political housecleaning. The man at the center of one of these purges was about as close to Stalin as a person could get. Sergei Kirov was the man Stalin seemed most likely to choose to take his place one day. Kirov was a Bolshevik Party leader, a famous speaker, and a favorite of Russian workers.

This did not make Kirov a real rival to Stalin, but the two men did disagree on a few key issues. Apparently that was enough to make him a threat in Stalin's mind. On December 1, 1934, in Leningrad, Kirov was assassinated—on orders issued by Stalin himself.

Stalin then blamed Kirov's death on other party members—hundreds of them. It was a massive conspiracy, Stalin claimed. Suddenly every Bolshevik Party member was a potential enemy of the people. Many would end up paying for Kirov's death.

THE GREAT PURGE

Stalin had used Kirov's death to invent enemies within his own party. In another purge he manipulated party members into doing the inventing for him. On July 29, 1936, Stalin announced: "The inalienable quality of every Bolshevik under present conditions should be the ability to recognize an enemy of the party no matter how well he may be masked."

In other words, Stalin fully expected loyal party members to accuse people of being disloyal who might not really be disloyal at all, and that wasn't all. To refuse to accuse anyone of disloyalty could put you yourself under suspicion. Suddenly everyone was looking at everyone else with suspicion and fear.

With this announcement, Stalin launched his Great Purge. So many people were branded as enemies in this series of purges that Stalin himself could not keep track of them all. Sometimes he would tell an associate to bring him a certain person he needed for a task, only to learn that this person was not available. Why? Stalin wanted to know. Because that person had been accused of disloyalty, found guilty, and executed.

THE POSSIBLE CRIME

Stalin's totalitarian reign featured the "show trial," a unique propaganda technique for inventing and exploiting enemies. In these highly publicized events, some defendants were accused of outright sabotage.

Others were on trial for so-called counter-revolutionary activities, a vague catchall term for doing or saying something that violated the party line.

Most of the defendants were chosen not because they actually had committed a crime but because they might have committed a crime or might commit one in the future. This type of offense was known as the "possible crime." Possible-crime suspects were chosen because of their background or personality. Somehow these factors suggested that they were capable of committing the crime they were charged with, which was enough to make them guilty.

Many of the show-trial defendants made public confessions, admitting to crimes they had not committed. Some did so because they were convinced it was their duty. The ones who refused were found guilty anyway.

INVENTED ENEMIES

One of these show trials, in 1936, involved the Kirov assassination. A total of fifteen party members confessed to being part of the supposed conspiracy. Some publicly confessed their guilt. Others signed false confessions that the party had written for them.

Some confessions were helped along by various torture tactics. One method was called the swan dive. Rope running between the victim's jaws and feet was tied firmly and tightened. Slowly the victim's back would arch more and more. If the victim still refused to confess, the rope was tightened until his back broke.

Stalin's show trials were staged to prove that the nation in general and Stalin's Bolshevik Party in particular were under constant fire from enemies within the nation. The trials helped convince the Soviet public that Stalin's extreme measures were both necessary and justified.

LABOR CAMPS

Some of Stalin's enemies were executed. Others were persecuted by being shut away from the rest of society in labor camps. Here is how writer Hannah Arendt described the life in these places:

> [T]he human masses sealed off in them are treated as if they no longer existed, as if what happened to them were no longer of any interest to anybody, as if they were already dead and some evil spirit gone mad were amusing himself

by stopping them for a while between life and death before admitting them to eternal peace.

Many peasants resisted Stalin's call for collective farming. Among them were the wealthier class of farmers, known as kulaks, many of whom ended up in these camps. After being declared "enemies of the people," millions of kulaks lost their land and homes and were stripped of their possessions, even their pots and pans. None of their friends or neighbors dared reach out to them. Stalin's law forbade anyone from aiding kulak families.

An estimated ten million kulaks were loaded onto railroad boxcars and transported to the camps. Many of these "special settlements," as the Communists called them, were located in the frigid wilderness of Siberia. Like the European Jews, many kulaks perished during the journey. Most of the survivors became slave laborers in the nearby mines and factories. Many died from the frigid temperatures and the harsh working and living conditions.

RESISTANCE AND RETALIATION

Stalin hoped that by punishing the kulaks he would strike enough terror into the hearts of the other peasants to stop them from resisting collective farming. He was wrong. Resistance was particularly strong in the Ukraine region of the Soviet Union. In 1932, Stalin sent dedicated young Communists out to the Ukrainian countryside to drum up support for his regime, thinking that propaganda might accomplish what terror alone could not.

Instead of support, the young Communists were greeted with resistance and outright rebellion. Ukrainian peasants were burning down their own homes rather than giving them up to the Communist collectives, and harassing and even assassinating local Soviet officials.

Stalin retaliated by using famine as a punishment. He increased the quota of crops that the Ukrainian peasants had to send out of the region and sent in some 100,000 soldiers to enforce the policy. They went from house to house seizing food. Soon, people began dropping dead in the streets from starvation. They killed and ate dogs, cats, birds, even mice. Finally, they resorted to eating trees and bushes.

News of the Ukrainian famine spread. Food supplies came from Europe, the United States, and Canada, but Soviet authorities would not allow it in. By the spring of 1933, an estimated 25,000 Ukrainians were dying of starvation each day.

STALIN'S DECLINE

Stalin's plans to industrialize and modernize the Soviet Union met with some success at first, but at a price. During the first ten years of collectivization, industrial output shot up but agricultural production fell, and famine killed millions. In 1937, a Soviet worker wrote this in a letter: "What is there to say about Soviet power? It's lies. . . . I am a worker, wear torn clothes, my four children go to school half-starving, in rags."

New cities were built around the big new Soviet factories, but the workers lived in cramped apartments and crowded dormitories. Others lived in huts made of sticks and mud. As living standards declined, crime rates rose. Meanwhile, Stalin failed to see that his ongoing purges of the educated classes helped doom his grand plan to failure. Arendt wrote:

> If the liquidation of classes (in the Soviet Union) made no political sense, it was positively disastrous for the Soviet economy. . . . The liquidation of the bureaucracy, that is, of the class of factory managers and engineers, finally deprived industrial enterprises of what little experience and know-how the new Russian technical intelligentsia had been able to acquire.

Stalin was still firmly in power when he died, in 1953, of a brain hemorrhage. By then he had managed to lead the Soviet Union to the position of a world military and industrial power. But those gains had come at a monstrous price. Estimates put the death toll under Stain's leadership at about twenty million people.

And what of Lenin's and Stalin's grand plan of a communist paradise-on-earth where people produced everything they needed in abundance? Instead of the nation's wealth being shared, most of it went into the pockets of Communist Party leaders and into the buildup of a massive military force. Meanwhile, the relatively low standard of living of the average Soviet citizen was little improved.

The End of Honor

In 1961, eight years after Stalin's death, his body was removed from its resting place next to Lenin's in the Kremlin mausoleum. The decree ordering the removal was read by Nikita Khrushchev, first secretary of the Communist Party and Soviet premier:

> The further retention in the mausoleum of the sarcophagus with the bier of J. V. Stalin shall be recognized as inappropriate since the serious violations by Stalin of Lenin's precepts, abuse of power, mass repressions against honorable Soviet people, and other activities in the period of the personality cult make it impossible to leave the bier with his body in the mausoleum of V. I. Lenin.

It was a quiet ceremony this time. There were no frantic, adoring crowds to watch as Stalin's body was reburied three hundred feet from Lenin's. A dark granite stone marking the grave read, simply: J. V. STALIN 1879–1953.

DE-STALINIZATION

Stalin's body was put on display in Moscow's Kremlin for three days. During his thirty years as a dictator Stalin had presided over the death of millions, yet thousands of Soviet citizens lined up outside in the snow in the hope of catching one last glimpse of his body. The adoring crowds pushed so hard that chaos erupted. People were trampled, crushed, and suffocated. An estimated 500 people were killed. After the viewing, Stalin's body was embalmed and placed in a glass-topped coffin in a tomb next to Lenin's.

During the years immediately following his death, the party line on Stalin changed drastically. He went from being the Father of Peoples and Lenin's able successor to the man responsible for the deaths of millions of his own people.

Meanwhile, Stalin's place as dictator was taken by a small group of party leaders led by Nikita Khrushchev, first secretary of the Communist Party and Soviet premier. The policies instituted by Khrushchev became known collectively as de-Stalinization. No more would Stalin be seen, officially at least, as a great leader.

DISSOLUTION OF THE SOVIET UNION

When Mikhail Gorbachev became the new Soviet leader, in 1985, he instituted a series of reforms that were supposed to liberalize and strengthen the nation. People regained some of the freedoms that Lenin, Stalin, and their successors had repressed, including private ownership of businesses.

These reforms were supposed to strengthen the Soviet Union, but they had the opposite effect. They encouraged the various Soviet republics, such as Estonia, Lithuania, and Ukraine, to strive for independence instead.

In 1990, the Central Committee of the Soviet Communist Party agreed to relinquish much of its power. One by one, fourteen of the Soviet republics became independent nations. By 1991, the Soviet Union had collapsed.

Today some of these fourteen independent republics are run by dictators. They include Turkmenistan, Belarus, and Uzbekistan. Since the 1991 breakup, Russia, formerly the dominant nation in the Soviet Union, has struggled to build a democratic political system.

11
Mao's Rise ■ ■ ■

MAO ZEDONG WAS BORN INTO A CHINESE peasant family in
1893. While working as a librarian in Beijing, he read the works of
Karl Marx and became a convert to Communism. He was present at
the first meeting of the Chinese Communist Party (CCP) in 1921. The
meeting was supported by the Soviet Union. Like Stalin, Mao took up
a revolutionary career as a labor organizer.

Until 1927, Mao and other Chinese Communists worked with the
Kuomintang, the party striving to unite China into a republic. Then
there came a violent split. The Kuomintang banished the communists
from the party and forced them to flee to the mountains of South China,
where they formed a guerrilla army supported by the local peasants.
Mao became one of the leaders of the army and of the CCP.

MAO AND MILITARY POWER
In 1934 the communist army, commanded by Mao and Zhou Enlai,
was in full retreat from the Kuomintang army, led by General Chiang
Kai-shek. The retreat would last more than a year and cover some
5,000 miles (8,000 kilometers) of rugged terrain in southern, western,
and northern China with the enemy harassing them all the way. The
communist army's retreat became known as the Long March.

Mao's troops numbered 100,000 at the beginning of the march. Tens
of thousands of communist troops died along the way, and the army was

driven to the brink of extinction. Thanks to a series of successful tactical moves engineered by Mao, 8,000 soldiers survived the journey.

Driven into isolation in the north of China, the survivors had time to rest and regroup. Despite the losses, Mao's military exploits gained him power within the CCP.

MAO PREVAILS

Mao Zedong took over leadership of the party in 1935. Fourteen years—mostly of war—followed, including a civil war with Mao's forces opposed by the anti-Communist forces of General Chiang Kai-shek. In 1949 communist forces emerged victorious, and Mao announced the founding of the People's Republic of China (PRC). Mao was credited with creating something that had not existed in more than a hundred years: a unified Chinese nation free of foreign influence.

The PRC was led by the CCP under a one-party system. As chairman of the party, Mao was now dictator of the most populous nation on Earth, and one of the poorest. China's 400 million people were mostly peasants, families of subsistence farmers who grew just enough to feed themselves. Eighty percent of the Chinese were illiterate. The average life expectancy was just thirty-five years.

MAO AND THE HUNDRED FLOWERS

How could the Chinese people's standard of living be improved? During the rare times when a dictator lets his guard down to encourage free expression, he may find that he has lost his all-important controlling grip on the people. Mao Zedong learned this lesson the hard way.

In the summer of 1956, Mao called upon the people for constructive criticism for improving life in China. "Let a hundred flowers bloom, let a hundred schools of thought contend," he declared.

This was the start of the Hundred Flowers Campaign. Sharing thoughts was vital, Mao announced. Everyone must participate. Anyone not expressing healthy criticism of the central government would come in for criticism himself.

At first hardly anyone responded. Many citizens were suspicious that this campaign amounted to a plot that would get them in trouble. Finally, though, the letters started coming in, a trickle at first, then a flood. In a seventeen-day period in June 1957, millions of letters poured in, and much of the criticism, to Mao's way of thinking, was neither healthy nor constructive. People criticized the CCP's harsh repression of intellectuals. They complained about China's low standards of living. They said that CCP members were corrupt.

Mao soon lost patience. This was not the affirmation of communism he had expected. So he abruptly ended this campaign and launched another: the Anti-Rightist Movement. He turned on those who had criticized the communist bureaucracy, even those who had offered healthy and constructive criticism. All were now seen as rightists, counter-revolutionaries, disloyal, bad elements. Mao had an estimated half-million of these Hundred Flowers letter writers rounded up and exiled to work camps to do slave labor.

A NEW SOCIETY

Mao decided that the only way to improve his nation was through a radical revolution that would overturn the most basic beliefs and traditions of Chinese culture, including the authority of elders, the authority of husbands over wives, and all religious traditions. Basic political structures had to be dismantled as well, including the family, the clan, and the state. All this must be swept away in the tide of revolution for a true communist society to be born.

In this new society, authority would be centralized in a structure Mao called the New Democracy. Banks and industry would have to be nationalized and land redistributed from wealthy landowners to poor peasants.

Except for its emphasis on farming and peasants as opposed to industry and factory workers, the basics and ideals of Maoism were similar to those of Leninism: Remake society by transferring power to a dictatorial central government that would make sure that everyone was treated fairly.

THE GREAT LEAP FORWARD

The peasants were the key to this revolution. In Mao's mind they possessed immense potential energy and strength, but those qualities had never been properly organized and fueled. People could not be expected to work effectively as mere individuals. They had to be organized by the state to work in groups for the good of all. Mao wrote:

> For thousands of years a system of individual production
> has prevailed among the peasant masses under which

a family or a household forms a productive unit. This scattered, individual form of production . . . has plunged the peasants into perpetual poverty. The only way to change this state of affairs is gradual collectivization.

In 1958, Mao launched the Great Leap Forward. The goal was to modernize China's economy so that within thirty years it would rival that of the United States. An inspired peasantry would soon transform this poor and backward country into a rich and modern Communist nation.

COMMUNES

Mao's key to collectivization was communes. The typical commune would contain about 5,000 families, all sharing their belongings. Everything, including tools and animals, would be owned by the commune, which would be supervised by the CCP.

The commune would provide workers and their families with all the essentials, including food, housing, and entertainment. There would be doctors, teachers, and other specialists to attend to every need. Schools, nurseries, and elderly care homes, known as "houses of happiness," took care of children and elderly relatives so that adults could concentrate on their work.

To make all this a reality, workers in each commune were organized into units, like soldiers in an army. A work team was composed of twelve families; a brigade was composed of twelve work teams; and so on. Each unit was assigned a certain kind of work to do and production quotas to meet. Communist Party members watched over each unit to see that everything went according to Chairman Mao's plan.

Within a year's time, Mao's nationwide revolutionary plan was in full operation. Some 700 million people had been taken from their homes and moved into communes. Like Hitler and Stalin, Mao had radically altered daily life in his nation.

12
Mao's Fall ■ ■ ■

MAO FIRMLY BELIEVED THAT THE MASSES, if united and energized by a common cause, could do almost anything. But could they move, in twenty years' time, from producing virtually no steel at all to producing more than the rest of the world combined? That was one goal of the Great Leap Forward.

To reach this lofty goal, Mao mobilized peasants in villages all over his nation. They were ordered to gather together all their cooking and farming equipment made of iron. It would be collected by the CCP and made into steel. To smelt all this iron for steel, Mao ordered trees all over China to be felled and made into charcoal.

UNINTENDED CONSEQUENCES

Caught up in his mission, Mao failed to attend to the possible consequences. So many trees were cut down that much of China was utterly deforested, which meant that for the next decade there would be very little wood around for the smelting of more iron.

Meanwhile, with all that agricultural equipment melted down, many farmers had nothing left with which to farm. So some 90 million peasants abandoned farming and moved into cities to take up factory work.

As a result, Chinese steel production soared, but with so much emphasis on quantity, quality had to suffer. China's steel was so low-

China's Red Guard carried out Mao's orders and terrorized their nation. In 1967, the Red Guard paraded through Beijing carrying a portrait of Mao Zedong and red flags.

grade that little of it could be used. Meanwhile, agricultural production plummeted. With so many farmers moving to cities and working in factories, grain, cotton, and other crops rotted in the fields. In 1959, famine swept the nation, and millions starved.

MAO'S CULTURAL REVOLUTION

After the disaster of the Great Leap Forward, Mao was forced to step down as CCP chairman. That position was taken on by Deng Xiaoping, who also took over management of China's economic affairs from Mao.

Mao saw his power slipping, so he and his supporters organized a youth militia known as the Red Guard. Their mission was to "re-educate" people about Mao's philosophy and goals to rally them back to his side.

But these youthful Guard members, many of whom were teenagers, were so zealously devoted to their leader that they began attacking people who, in their eyes, were not loyal enough. No one was exempt. To show their own loyalty, some Guard members actually targeted their parents. One of their chants was "Don't love father, don't love mother, just love the country."

Mao did not tell the Red Guard to moderate their efforts, not even when their punishments turned cruel, humiliating, and bizarre. Some victims were forced to strip naked and march through town for all to see. Others had to chew on chunks of shattered glass.

The Guard's fanatical crusade flung the People's Republic of China into chaos. Schools and universities were forced to close their doors, and the economy suffered. In October 1968, when Mao's chief CCP rival, Liu Shao-chi, was expelled from the party, Mao decided that the Cultural Revolution could end. By then, estimates of the number of people who died at the hands of the Red Guard ran into the millions.

MAO'S END

Mao Zedong died of a heart attack in 1976, leaving behind scores of dead and hungry people. Estimates of the death toll from Mao's Great Leap Forward reached 20 million. Dictators have a way of refusing to face the truth. When Mao heard this estimate, he strongly disagreed. "How could we possibly kill 20 million people?" he asked.

On the day of Mao's death, estimates say that some 200 million Chinese suffered from malnutrition—20 percent of the population. Experts blame the failure of Mao's collective farming policy and the

Quotations from Chairman Mao

Mao's Red Guard carried copies of *Quotations from Chairman Mao Zedong* or, as the pocket-sized edition was known in the West, Mao's *Little Red Book*, a collection of quotes from his writings and speeches. The book was a major part of Mao's cult of personality. All over China, people carried copies of the book and quoted passages from it. Here are some examples:

> Every Communist must grasp the truth, Political power grows out of the barrel of a gun.

> A revolution is not a dinner party, or writing an essay, or painting a picture, or doing embroidery; it cannot be so refined, so leisurely and gentle, so temperate, kind, courteous, restrained and magnanimous. A revolution is an insurrection, an act of violence by which one class overthrows another.

> We should support whatever the enemy opposes and oppose whatever the enemy supports.

> The masses have boundless creative power. They can organize themselves and concentrate on places and branches of work where they can give full play to their energy; they can concentrate on production in breadth and depth and create more and more undertakings for their own well-being.

> In order to build a great socialist society, it is of the utmost importance to arouse the broad masses of women to join in productive activity. Men and women must receive equal pay for equal work in production. Genuine equality between the sexes can only be realized in the process of the socialist transformation of society as a whole.

During Mao's Cultural Revolution, Guard members would harass citizens who had fallen out of favor with the CCP by demanding that they produce the *Quotations* on the spot. Citizens who failed were liable to be beaten or sentenced to years of hard labor or imprisonment.

economic chaos caused by the Cultural Revolution.

However, during his reign as dictator, Mao, like Stalin, transformed his nation into a major military and industrial power. Soon after Mao's death, though, the CCP announced that henceforth China would move in other directions, and the new regime quickly began reversing Mao's policies.

CHINA AFTER MAO

After Mao, China's government remained authoritarian, but instead of a dictator, a small group of CCP leaders held control. One of them, Deng Xiaoping, delivered a speech to the 1977 CCP Congress that called for the modernization of agriculture, industry, science and technology, and the military.

Mao had depended almost entirely upon the Chinese themselves to supply the know-how and capital to modernize China. China's new leaders reached outside the nation. Their Ten-Year Plan called for using foreign investment and know-how to help reach production goals. For example, Germany and Japan built major steel plants in China. The plan also called for a huge investment in agriculture. To meet these demands, China borrowed billions of dollars from foreign banks.

China's economic reforms since 1978 have helped millions of people rise from poverty. In just two decades, from 1981 to 2001, the proportion of China's population living below the poverty line fell from 53 percent to 8 percent.

Individual freedoms are another matter. The PRC Constitution guarantees basic freedoms, including freedom of speech and the press. Yet the CCP routinely censors speech and protests from organizations that it feels threatens the nation's stability. In 1989 this attitude led to the Tiananmen Square protests, a widely reported series of student demonstrations against CCP policies. Government crackdowns led to the deaths of protestors.

The PRC government continues to run China's state media. As for foreign media, the party attempts to control TV and radio broadcasts reaching China as well as Internet sites and the distribution of foreign newspapers. As China's economy continues to grow, though, personal freedoms may grow as well.

As the nation's standard of living keeps rising, Mao's memory keeps fading away. China's leaders are promoting a more peaceful, less chaotic version of the nation's history, which has no room for Mao

Zedong. As of 2006, Mao had been all but eliminated from China's official version of its past. The history textbook used for Shanghai's junior and senior high school students, for instance, mentioned Mao Zedong only once—in a chapter on etiquette.

13
Modern Dictators ■ ■ ■

THE THREE TOWERING TOTALITARIAN dictators of the twentieth century are gone. But totalitarianism did not die with Hitler, Stalin, and Mao. Totalitarian governments continue to rule troubled nations. North Korea is one.

Occasionally a totalitarian dictator's son succeeds him in office. Kim Il-sung was North Korea's communist dictator from 1948 until his death in 1994. Four years later his son, Kim Jong-il, took over.

Kim Jong-il maintains a totalitarian stranglehold on North Korea's politics, economy, and cultural life, using propaganda to keep the grip tight. He has used it to create an elaborate cult of personality, which begins with the moment of his birth.

THE CULT OF PERSONALITY

The real Kim Jong-il was born in Siberia, in the former Soviet Union. But in the fictitious world he has made up for the public, he was born in a log cabin near the top of North Korea's highest mountain. And to herald this earthshaking event, a double rainbow and a bright star appeared in the heavens.

Kim is well known for his pompous self-regard. North Korean media hail him as the "peerless leader," and his image is everywhere. Typical photos show him with a puffy permed hairdo. He is known

Dictator Kim Jong-il of North Korea uses propaganda to retain his total power.

to wear platform shoes to add several inches to his height of 5 feet 3 inches (160 centimeters).

Kim is also famous for his insatiable hunger for obedience and admiration. Even his imprisoned enemies must demonstrate their love for him. A former inmate in one of Kim's prison camps says:

> The prisoners are instructed to memorize fifteen officially designated songs praising Kim Jong-il and sing the songs on the way to work, and while working. They are beaten if they do not sing loud enough and a brief pause in singing is taken as an indication of political discontent. The prisoners must sing the songs as loudly as possible even though they are usually very tired.

Kim Jong-il's communist government maintains tight control of the nation's news media, using them to build up his cult of personality. According to North Korean propaganda, their leader is vastly famous and admired worldwide. As evidence, North Korean television proudly reports what leaders from nations around the world are supposedly saying about their leader.

These heads of state have allegedly heaped dozens of admiring titles upon Kim. Some titles praise his courage and leadership skills: World's Best Ideal Leader with Versatile Talents, Supreme Commander at the Forefront of the Struggle Against Imperialism and the United States, Guardian Deity of the Planet.

Some focus on his creative talents: Power Incarnate with Endless Creativity; Humankind's Greatest Musical Genius; Master of Literature, Arts, and Architecture; World's Greatest Writer.

Other titles salute his intelligence: Man with Encyclopedic Knowledge, Best Leader Who Realized Human Wisdom, Perfect Picture of Wisdom and Boldness.

Still others depict him as super-human: Greatest Saint, Heaven-Sent Hero, Present-day God.

WEAPONS VERSUS FOOD

Has Kim used his absolute power and godlike status to better his people's lives? Like Hitler, Stalin, and Mao, he has gone to great lengths to build up his nation's armed forces. It is estimated that although North Korea ranks forty-ninth in world population, with about 23 million people, it has the world's fourth-largest largest army. In 2006, North Korea began test-firing nuclear missiles, suggesting that Kim's nation may be on its way to becoming a serious threat to the world.

Putting weapons first is a risky move for a nation as poor as North Korea. Other segments of the economy are bound to suffer. Throughout Kim's reign, his nation has suffered life-threatening food shortages. Without aid from foreign nations, North Korea would not be able to feed its people.

These chronic food shortages have another cause besides military spending. Kim's agricultural program is based on collective farming practices similar to Stalin's and Mao's. Kim's father also insisted on collective farming, with similar drastic results. In 1991 things got so desperate that Kim Il-sung launched a "let's eat two meals a day" campaign.

JONG-IL'S UNREAL REALITY

But like other totalitarian dictators, no matter how severely his people suffer, Kim Jong-il refuses to change direction. Instead of altering his plan to correct the problem, he denies that the problem exists. All through the 1990s and into the twenty-first century, the North Korean government has used propaganda to create a fictitious North Korea that has no food shortages and no need of outside help.

North Korea is a highly secretive nation. Rarely are foreign visitors allowed. And those who do visit must be accompanied by government guides trained to explain things in terms of their leader's worldview.

The guides are ever-present, even during shopping trips and meals. North Korea's stores are usually empty because there are few goods available for purchase and little money with which to buy them. But a visiting reporter was told that "This shop is empty because it's a holiday." Lack of electricity is a constant problem, and blackouts are common even in the capital city of Pyongyang. When the reporter's meal in a Pyongyang restaurant was interrupted by a blackout, the guide explained, "The lights have gone off because it makes a more romantic atmosphere for dinner."

Citizens must share in Jong-il's fictitious reality—or suffer the consequences. Amnesty International (AI) is a worldwide organization campaigning for human rights. According to AI, the North Korean government "prevents the swift and equitable distribution of [food] aid, while the population is denied the right to freedom of movement, which would enable people to go and search for food."

AI cites reports that hungry North Koreans have been arrested, tortured, and even executed for stealing crops or livestock and for crossing the border into China to look for food. Kim Jong-il's government controls the media and guards its nation's borders to keep citizens from hearing news and opinions that contradict Jong-il's worldview.

Does Kim really believe his private version of reality? Other nations, including the United States, have openly questioned his sanity, a question that North Korean government sources refuse to answer.

HUSSEIN'S RISE

Iraq's Saddam Hussein was another modern totalitarian dictator. He came to power in 1973 with a mission in mind: to unite the various Arab-Islamic countries in the Middle East into one vast nation and drive out all Western influences. He also wished to modernize his nation and turn it into a socialist state.

But soon after taking control, Hussein abandoned his sense of mission. He resorted instead to having his enemies imprisoned. Long before Hussein rose to power, Iraq was a troubled, fractured nation. People were split along religious, ethnic, cultural, and class lines. So Hussein already had a host of enemies identified.

They included the Shi'a, the nation's dominant Islam sect, and the Kurds, an ethnic minority originally from eastern Turkey. He persecuted these enemies so ruthlessly that other world nations, including the United States, punished Iraq with economic sanctions. They refused to buy oil from his oil-rich nation. These sanctions helped keep Iraqi citizens' standard of living low. But Hussein would not back down. He refused to ease up on his enemies, and so the sanctions continued.

HUSSEIN'S DOWNFALL

Saddam Hussein's aggression extended beyond Iraq's borders. Rather than trying to unite Arab countries, he attacked them: first Iran in the Iraq-Iran War (1980–1988) and then Kuwait in the Persian Gulf War (1991). His efforts to conquer these neighboring nations were no more successful than his efforts to modernize and enrich his nation.

Like other totalitarian dictators, Hussein created a cult of personality to help keep him in power. All over Iraq, statues, posters, and murals honored him.

Hussein took special care to have himself depicted in various costumes and clothing. That way, it was hoped, all factions of Iraqi society would see him as one of them. Sometimes he was shown in the role of the devout Muslim, wearing traditional robes and praying toward Mecca. Other times he appeared in the role of the world leader, wearing Western-style suits. He was even depicted wearing clothing of the Kurds, the people he persecuted the most.

In 2003 the United States invaded and occupied Iraq. In the process they captured Hussein, ending his totalitarian reign. Hussein was executed in Iraq on December 30, 2006 for his crimes against humanity.

NEW AND TROUBLED NATIONS

Imagine how people would feel if their nation were controlled by a dominating foreign power that ruthlessly exploited its economy. Beginning in the nineteenth century, this is what happened to most of the countries on the African continent. Great Britain, Spain, France, and other highly developed Western European nations turned these African countries into colonies in order to profit from their natural resources. This practice became known as colonialism and imperialism.

Starting about 1960, these African colonies began demanding their freedom from European imperialism, and they soon got it. Suddenly they were independent nations, free to run their own economies and create their own governments for the first time in centuries.

Since then, during their more than forty years of independence, many of these nations have undergone violent revolutions and civil wars. Some still suffer hard economic times, which many Africans blame on the Western nations that occupied these countries and exploited their resources for so many years.

In short, they became the troubled sorts of nations that often end up in the hands of dictators. And that is just what has happened to many of these nations, about thirty in all, from Angola to Zimbabwe, at some time during their period of independence.

CASHING IN

Most of Africa's dictators since the 1960s fall into the authoritarian category. Authoritarian dictators are tyrannical but they stop short of being truly totalitarian. They have less grand, more limited plans in mind. They focus on improving their own lives: holding onto their power and cashing in on it by any means possible.

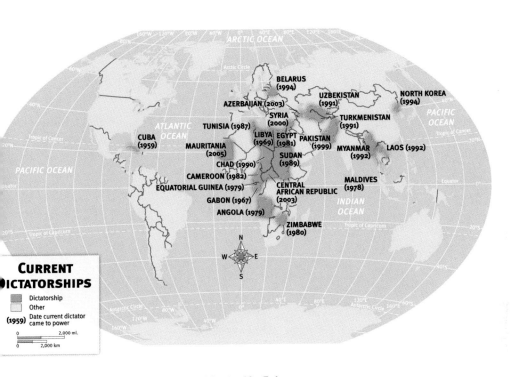

Dictatorships Today

Liberian President Charles Taylor sits on a throne with a traditional
dancer sitting at his feet during a ceremony in Monrovia where he was
crowned Chief Okatakyie, "The Greatest of Warriors." He was forced
from power in 2003.

Some cash in by following in the footsteps of the colonial powers that exploited their nation's resources for centuries. One of Liberia's most valuable natural resources is diamonds. During his six years as dictator, Charles Taylor grabbed much of Liberia's income from the diamond trade, using criminals to help him. The United Nations accused Taylor of recruiting thugs and terrorists from around the world to establish a criminal empire in West Africa. His actions helped propel Liberia into civil war. Taylor was forced from power in 2003.

Other authoritarian dictators cash in by looting the nation's treasury. General Sani Abacha was Nigeria's dictator from 1993 until his death five years later. During those years he and his family helped themselves to billions of dollars from the nation's treasury. Abacha also took advantage of international loans from the World Bank and the International Monetary Fund. These organizations lend money to help poor countries strengthen their economies. Abacha managed to divert some of these funds to his own private bank accounts.

Jean-Bédel Bokassa was dictator of the Central African Republic from 1966 to 1979. In 1976 he proclaimed himself emperor. His coronation ceremony cost the nation $30 million. It included an 11-foot-high, two ton, gold-plated, eagle-shaped throne. Bokassa's personal wealth was estimated at $125 million.

And the list goes on, one dictator after another plundering his nation's wealth. Instead of helping to solve the problems of these developing nations, most of Africa's post-colonial dictators just keep making matters worse.

SEIZING AND HOLDING POWER

The African dictators mentioned above all came to power by military coup. Each one led an armed uprising to depose the ruling head of state and his political party. Having taken power through force, they then use force to stay in power.

The results can be brutal. Abacha had nine of his political enemies executed simply for being opponents. Amnesty International reported that Taylor's forces used rape and torture to terrorize citizens. To put down an uprising against him, Bokassa was reported to have driven a truck over the bodies of schoolchildren.

Sometimes dictators allow elections to be held. But being dictators, they are free to use openly crooked campaign tactics that candidates in democratic nations would have a hard time getting away with.

A Tyrant's Ruined City

Mobutu Sese Seko, Zaire's former dictator, was born in Gbadolite, a small town in the rain forest, far from the nation's capital of Kinshasa. In the 1970s he honored his birthplace by erecting a series of palaces there.

Today Zaire has been renamed and Mobutu is dead, but the palaces remain as a reminder of the late dictator's colossal greed. In the 1980s his personal fortune was estimated at $4 billion. A good piece of it went into the building of what one visitor called "this Oz-like city . . . in a remote rain forest."

There is a village of Chinese pagodas with jade roofs and ponds. There is a marble mansion with two swimming pools and a fountain. There are three massive palaces.

But today the ponds are clotted with layer upon layer of green algae. The swimming pools and fountains are overgrown with creeping vines. The veranda below the balcony where Mobutu would speak to crowds of visitors is littered with broken glass. The vast palaces have all been looted. Goats roam them now.

Today most of Gbadolite's downtown buildings are deserted. Each day the surrounding rain forest grows inward to cover more of the town. Meanwhile, most of the Congolese people still live in huts of sticks and grass.

Robert Mugabe has been Zimbabwe's leader since 1980, when he gained office by popular vote. Mugabe was a well-liked president for a while. Then his regime turned dictatorial. In the 2002 election it looked like his chief opponent would win. So Mugabe's police beat up opposition voters and urged election officials to falsify results—and Mugabe won. In the 2005 election most polling stations were run by the dictator's troops. They told voters that only Mugabe supporters would get government food aid. With half of Zimbabwe's population in danger of starvation, voting for Mugabe's rival could be fatal. Again, Mugabe held onto power.

DRIVE OUT THE WEST

Mobutu Sese Seko ruled Zaire, now the Democratic Republic of the Congo, from 1965 to 1997. He also came to power by a military coup.

As dictator, Mobutu pledged to modernize the country and raise his people's standard of living. But not by turning his nation into an African version of a Western nation, he vowed. Mobutu pledged to erase all traces of Western influence and return his country to its authentic African origins. In a speech to the United Nations, he said: "Authenticity is the realization by the Zairean people that [Zaire] must return to its origins, seek out the values of its ancestors, to discover those which contribute to its harmonious and natural development. It is the refusal to blindly embrace imported ideologies."

At first Mobutu seemed serious and confident about his mission. As a sign of determination, he renamed himself Mobutu Sese Seko Kuku Ngbendu wa za Banga, which was officially translated to "the all-powerful warrior who, because of his endurance and inflexible will to win, will go from conquest to conquest leaving fire in his wake."

But as the years passed the Zairean dictator spent less time directing the nation's affairs and more time at one of his luxurious retreats far outside the capital. Mobutu lost his sense of mission and dedicated himself to plundering the nation's wealth instead, while its economy and citizens continued to suffer.

14
Fighting Tyrants

What strategies are world leaders employing to slow down and, hopefully, bring an eventual end to the destruction done by dictators? After the defeat of the brutal totalitarian dictatorships of World War II, a human rights movement began. The United Nations (UN) and its member states crafted several human rights treaties. One was the 1948 Convention on the Prevention and Punishment of the Crime of Genocide. Here is how the treaty defines genocide:

> "In the present Convention, genocide means any of the following acts committed with intent to destroy, in whole or in part, a national, ethnical, racial or religious group, as such:
>
> (a) Killing members of the group;
> (b) Causing serious bodily or mental harm to members of the group;
> (c) Deliberately inflicting on the group conditions of life calculated to bring about its physical destruction in whole or in part;
> (d) Imposing measures intended to prevent births within the group;
> (e) Forcibly transferring children of the group to another group."

The treaty goes on to state that "Persons committing genocide . . . shall be punished, whether they are constitutionally responsible rulers, public officials or private individuals." To deal with these perpetrators, the UN set up international courts. The first was the International Court of Justice (ICJ), also known as the World Court, established in 1945.The Court deals with non-human-rights issues as well, such as border and maritime disputes. It is located in The Hague, the capital of the Netherlands.

DICTATORS ON TRIAL

In 1993 the UN created another court to deal with perpetrators of genocide, the International Criminal Tribunal (ICT), also located in The Hague. Former Serbian dictator Slobodan Milošević went on trial at the ICT in 2002. He was charged with sixty-six counts of war crimes and crimes against humanity and genocide. These crimes were committed during the armed conflicts in Bosnia and Herzegovina, Croatia, and Kosovo, all parts of the former Yugoslavia, in the 1990s. Milošević's trial was cut short in 2006 when he died in his prison cell of heart-related illness. As of 2006, Liberia's Charles Taylor was also due to stand trial before the ICT. He faces eleven counts of war crimes and crimes against humanity involving some 250,000 deaths.

Dictators are sometimes tried in courts in their own nation. In 2006 Saddam Hussein was tried and found guilty by a court in Baghdad, Iraq, for crimes against humanity, including the jailing, torture, and executions of 148 Shi'ite villagers in 1982 and an attempt in 1988 to annihilate Iraq's Kurdish minority. In December 2006, he was executed for his crimes.

Campaigns are always under way to indict more former dictators for corruption and crimes against humanity. As of 2006, these former dictators included Chile's Augusto Pinochet Agarte, Chad's Hissene Habre, Indonesia's Haji Mohammad Suharto, and Uruguay's Juan Maria Bordaberry.

THE LESSER OF TWO EVILS

If relations between nations were less complicated and more clear-cut, the fight against tyranny might be more effective than it has been. But international politics is a complex and sometimes bewildering phenomenon. Democratic nations often find themselves supporting brutal tyrants, helping them rise to power and remain there, then later

Iraq's dictator, Saddam Hussein, was executed in December 2006 for his brutal actions during his regime.

fighting to pull them back down. Why would a democratic nation behave in such contrary ways?

There is a principle known as "the lesser of two evils." Sometimes a democratic nation finds itself faced with two bad political choices and no good ones. If one of these bad choices is less bad than the other, the nation must make that less-bad choice.

The lesser-of-two-evils principle sometimes comes into play when democracies must deal with dictators. This was especially true during the Cold War years (1945–1991), when the United States, with its democratic government, and the Soviet Union, with its communist government, were bitter enemies.

SUPPORT FOR DICTATORS

Saddam Hussein was a dictator who benefited from this Cold War strife. In the mid–1970s the United States supported his rise to power in Iraq in order to counter the rise of Iraq's Communist party. The United States preferred an anti-communist dictator to a communist government in Iraq.

Thirty years later the Soviet Union had collapsed, and U.S. leaders had shifted their attentions. Instead of communism, they now saw terrorism as the most dire threat to democracy. And they saw Saddam Hussein as a supporter of terrorism. So in 2003, U.S. troops invaded Iraq and brought down the dictator they once had helped rise to power.

Ngo Dinh Diem was another lesser-of-two-evils choice. Diem was South Vietnam's dictator during the early part of the Vietnam War. During that civil war (1965–1973), South Vietnam fought North Vietnam, which was headed by Ho Chi Minh's communist regime. Though Diem's regime was known to be brutal, the United States supported him. They saw Diem as less evil than his communist counterpart in the north.

FINAL WORDS

What is the extent of the human damage done by dictators? According to sociologist Daniel Chirot, well over 100 million people have died as a result of war and political repression during the last hundred years.

But only about half died in military battles. The other 50 million

Castro Must Go

In 1959, following the Cuban Revolution, Fidel Castro became Cuba's president, suspended the constitution, and set up a Soviet-style dictatorship with strict limitations on human rights. This was at the height of the Cold War, and having a communist nation just ninety miles off Florida's southern tip led by a dictator who kept delivering anti-American speeches made U.S. leaders uneasy.

From 1960 to 1965, the Central Intelligence Agency, the U.S. secret agency responsible for spying on other nations, tried again and again to eliminate Castro. A CIA-led invasion of Cuba in 1962 failed, as did plots to assassinate the Cuban dictator.

According to unofficial sources, the plots included some unusual weapons. Since Castro was famous for smoking cigars, CIA agents reportedly planned to slip him poisoned panatellas. When agents discovered the location of a spot off the Cuban coast where Castro often swam, they thought of mining the water with exploding clam shells. Usually, Castro wore a wetsuit when he swam, so agents considered sending a spy to infect it with deadly bacteria. Castro was famous for his long beard. Supposedly, agents cooked up a plot to slip poisoned foot powder into his shoes that would make his hair fall out.

Did any of these offbeat plans ever get put into action? No one can say because the information surrounding Castro and the CIA is still officially secret. But if they ever did, the plans failed. As of 2006, the eighty-year-old dictator remained in power, though diagnosed with terminal cancer.

were civilians killed by persecution and abuse. Then there are the several billion people who have survived being terrorized and persecuted by the leaders of tyrannical regimes.

Today dozens of tyrannical dictators remain in power around the world for the same reasons they always have. There are still troubled nations whose people suffer from marginal standards of living, internal strife, and little in the way of hope. And there are still self-assured power-seekers such as Kim Jong-il to take charge and rule them with false promises, impossible hopes, propaganda, and terror. This tyrannical form of government appears destined to remain a prominent part of the world's political landscape.

Dictatorship and Other Governments

DICTATORSHIP	COMMUNISM	SOCIALISM
Often only one legal political party	Only one legal political party (Communist Party)	Multiple legal political parties; limited electoral freedom
Limited or no electoral freedom	No free elections; rule by a single individual or small group	Rule by people through elections, although individual or small group may dominate politics
Rule by a single individual; opposition and dissent are limited or forbidden	Opposition and dissent are limited or forbidden	Opposition and dissent may be limited
Limited property rights	No private property	Limited property rights
Government may have significant role in economy	State-controlled economy	Government has significant role in economy
Unemployment determined by combination of the free market and government policy	Officially no unemployment	Unemployment determined by combination of the free market and government policy
Some religious freedom, if it does not threaten the regime	No freedom of religion	May have religious freedom
Limited or no civil rights; welfare programs are limited	Limited or no civil liberties or civil rights; widespread social welfare programs (such as free education, health care, and housing)	Civil liberties and civil rights may be curtailed by government, especially economic rights; widespread social welfare programs (such as free education, health care, and housing)

DEMOCRACY	MONARCHY*	THEOCRACY
Multiple legal political parties	May have no legal political parties, or only one	Often only one legal political party
Free, open rule by the people through elections	Limited or no electoral freedom; rule by a single individual; monarchy may be hereditary or elective	Limited or no electoral freedom; rule by a single individual or small group
Opposition and dissent are accepted and may be encouraged	Opposition and dissent may be limited or forbidden	Opposition and dissent are limited or forbidden
Private property protected by law and constitution	Limited property rights, usually inherited; monarch may claim ownership of entire kingdom	Limited property rights
Economy determined by free market	Government may have significant role in economy	Government may be have a significant role in economy
Unemployment determined mainly by the free market	Monarch may determine how people are to be employed; forced labor may be required	Unemployment determined by free market and government policy
Freedom of religion	Religious freedom may be allowed if it does not threaten the regime, or not, depending on ruler	Religious worship limited to the state religion
widespread and comprehensive civil liberties and civil rights; some social welfare	Social welfare programs may be limited	Limited or no civil liberties or civil rights; social welfare programs are limited

*Monarchy here refers to absolute monarchy, the traditional form of monarchy known in many earlier kingdoms but rare today; modern constitutional monarchies are monarchies in name only and are typically governed as democratic or socialist republics.

Timeline of Dictators

Gaius Julius Caesar
501 BCE
Office of dictator originates in Ancient Rome

100 BCE
Caesar born to wealthy Roman family

59 BCE
Caesar elected senior consul of the Roman Republic

45 BCE
After a series of military victories, Caesar is proclaimed dictator for life

44 BCE
Caesar assassinated; office of dictator abolished

Genghis Khan
1165
Khan born in steppes region of Mongolia

1206
Khan proclaimed ruler of Mongolia

1215
Khan conquers Xi Xia region of China

1222
Khan conquers Khwarazmian empire in Central Asia

1227
Khan dies, leaving empire to his four sons

Lorenzo di Piero de Medici
1449
Lorenzo born in Florence, Italy, to Medicis, powerful family of bankers and patrons of the arts

1469
Lorenzo becomes Florence's unofficial dictator

1478
Lorenzo negotiates with King of Naples to avoid war

1492
Lorenzo dies without realizing his ambition of unifying Northern Italy

Toyotomi Hideyoshi
1536
Hideyoshi born in Japan's Owari Province

1582
Hideyoshi named Japan's civilian dictator; begins instituting legal reforms and unifying Japan

1588
Hideyoshi disarms the peasants, helping to establish domestic peace

1598
Hideyoshi dies; his rivals assume his power but keep many of his reforms intact

Napoleon Bonaparte
1769
Bonaparte born on the island of Corsica

1789
French Revolution begins

1795
Bonaparte gathers fame and power by defeating Royalists during French Revolution

1798
Bonaparte leads French army in invasion of Egypt

1799
Bonaparte becomes France's military dictator, ending the French Revolution

1804

Bonaparte crowned France's emperor; his Napoleonic Codes are approved

1814

Bonaparte falls from power and France returns to monarchy

1821

Bonaparte dies on the island of St. Helena while in exile

Porfirio Díaz

1830

Díaz born in Oaxaca, Mexico

1855

Díaz, a military commander, helps overthrow dictator Santa Anna

1876

Díaz becomes Mexico's dictator by military coup; seen as champion of the poor

1876–1911

Díaz's policies help modernize Mexico but do not help the poor

1910

Díaz overthrown by rebels as Mexican Revolution begins

Adolf Hitler

1889

Hitler born in Austria

1914–1918

Hitler serves in Bavarian Army in World War I

1921

Hitler assumes leadership of Nazi Party

1933

Hitler appointed German chancellor; Enabling Act passed, giving Hitler and his Nazi Party increased powers

1934

Hitler becomes Germany's totalitarian dictator for life

1939

Hitler orders invasion of Czechoslovakia, with invasions and occupations of other European nations to follow, signaling start of World War II
    Nazis begin setting up European ghettos as part of Hitler's planned genocide of the Jews

1942

Nazis begin deporting Jews from ghettos to concentration camps, where some six million of them will perish

1945

Nazis defeated by Allied forces; Hitler is thought to commit suicide

Joseph Stalin
1879

Stalin born in Soviet state of Georgia

1917

Russian Revolution takes place, with Communist forces led by Vladimir Lenin winning

1928

Stalin takes over Communist Party leadership following Lenin's death the year before and becomes Soviet Union's totalitarian dictator; launches series of Five-Year Plans to modernize the nation

1930s

Stalin's plans for collective farming lead to a series of famines in which millions die

1936

Stalin launches the Great Purge, in which Communist Party members not in Stalin's favor are persecuted, imprisoned in work camps, or executed

1944

Soviet troops are instrumental in bringing about Germany's defeat in World War II

1953

Stalin dies, bringing his quarter-century of dictatorship to an end, during which the Soviet Union was transformed into a world military and industrial power

1956

Soviet leader Nikita Khrushchev denounces Stalin, helping pave the way for "de-Stalinization" of the Soviet Union

Mao Zedong

1893

Mao born to a peasant family in China's Hunan Province

1921

Mao joins the Chinese Communist Party (CCP)

1935

Mao takes over leadership of the CCP

1949

Mao announces founding of the People's Republic of China and becomes the nation's totalitarian dictator

1958

Mao launches the Great Leap Forward, to modernize China, based on collective farming and communes

1959

Mao's Great Leap Forward fails as famine sweeps the land

1965

Mao launches the Cultural Revolution to gain back lost power

1968

Mao announces the end of the chaotic Cultural Revolution

1976

Mao dies, having led China toward becoming a world military and industrial power

NOTES

Chapter 2

p. 16, par. 6, "Mongols." Wikipedia. en.wikipedia.org/wiki/Mongols

p. 17, par. 2, "Genghis Khan." NationalGeographic.com. 1997. military-history.about.com/gi/dynamic/offsite.htm?zi=1/XJ&sdn=military history&zu=http%3A%2F%2Fwww.nationalgeographic.com%2F genghis%2Ftimeline%2Findex.html

p. 17, par. 8, "Lorenzo the Magnificent." Buzzle.com. 2004. www.buzzle. com/editorials/4-19-2004-53113.asp

p. 19, Machiavelli, Niccolai. *The Prince*. 1532. www.gutenberg.org/ files/1232/1232-h/1232-h.htm

p. 24, par. 2, "Napoleon in Egypt." Discovery Channel. 1999. www.exn. ca/napoleon/egypt.cfm

p. 24, par. 6, Burnham, Robert, ed. "The Napoleon Series: The Civil Code." 2005. www.napoleon-series.org/research/government/c_ code.html

p. 27, "Napoleon Bonaparte Farewell to the Old Guard." The History Place, Great Speeches Collection. www.historyplace.com/speeches/ napoleon.htm

p. 30, par. 2, Tuck, Jim. "Democrat to Autocrat: The Transformation of Porfirio Díaz." Mexico Connect. www.mexconnect.com/mex_/history/jtuck/jtporfDíaz.html

Chapter 3

p. 34, par. 5, Galton, Francis. "Hereditary Genius: Prefatory Chapter to the Edition of 1892." galton.org/books/hereditary-genius/preface-2nd-ed.htm.

p. 34, par. 5, Ridley, Matt. *Genome: The Autobiography of a Species in 23 Chapters.* New York: HarperCollins, 1999, p. 289.

p. 34, par. 5, Fukuyama, Francis. *Our Posthuman Future: Consequences of the Biotechnology Revolution.* New York: Farrar, Straus & Giroux, 2002, p. 85.

Chapter 4

p. 37, par. 3, Hitler, Adolf. *Mein Kampf,* Vol. 1, Chapter 2. www.hitler.org/writings/Mein_Kampf/mkv1ch02.html

p. 38, par. 1, Hitler, Adolf. *Mein Kampf,* Vol. 1, Chapter 1.www.hitler.org/writings/Mein_Kampf/mkv1ch01.html

p. 39, par. 2, Hitler, Adolf. *Mein Kampf,* Vol. 1, Chapter 1. www.hitler.org/writings/Mein_Kampf/mkv1ch01.html

p. 39, par. 3, Hitler, Adolf. *Mein Kampf,* Vol. 1, Chapter 1. www.hitler.org/writings/Mein_Kampf/mkvch01.html

p. 39, par. 4, Hitler, Adolf. *Mein Kampf,* Vol. 1, Chapter 2. www.hitler.org/writings/Mein_Kampf/mkv1ch02.html

p. 41, par. 7, "Hitler's Enabling Act." The History Place. www.historyplace.com/worldwar2/timeline/enabling.htm

p. 43, par. 1, Arendt, Hannah. *The Origins of Totalitarianism.* New York: Harvest Books, 1985.

p. 45, par. 2, Hitler, Adolf. *Mein Kampf*, Vol. 1, Chapter 2. www.hitler. org/writings/Mein_Kampf/mkv1ch02.html

Chapter 5

p. 47, par. 2, "German Propaganda Archive." Calvin College. www. calvin.edu/academic/cas/gpa/ley2.htm

p. 48, par. 6, Furlong, Ray. "Events Mark Nazi Book-burning." BBC News, May 10, 2003. http://news.bbc.co.uk/go/pr/fr/-/1/hi/world/ europe/3016567.stm

p. 49, par. 4, Riefenstahl, Leni, director. *Triumph of the Will*, 1933.

p. 49, par. 5, "Triumph of the Will." The History Place. 2001. www. historyplace.com/worldwar2/triumph/tr-will.htm

p. 49, par. 6, Overy, Richard. The Dictators: Hitler's Germany, Stalin's Russia. New York: W. W. Norton, 2004, p. 19.

p. 49, par. 7–p.50, par. 1, "Triumph of the Will." The History Place. 2001. www.historyplace.com/worldwar2/triumph/tr-will.htm

p. 50, par. 2, "Triumph of the Will." The History Place. 2001. www. historyplace.com/worldwar2/triumph/tr-will.htm

p. 50, par. 4, "Dictator." FactBook.org. www.factbook.org/wikipedia/ en/d/di/dictator.html

p. 50, par. 5, Arendt, Hannah. *The Origins of Totalitarianism*. New York: Harvest Books, 1985, p. 418.

p. 50, par. 5, Overy, Ibid., p. 21.

p. 50, par. 6, "Rudolf Hess, Biography." The History Place. www. historyplace.com/worldwar2/biographies/hess-bio.htm

p. 50, par. 7–p. 51, par. 1, Overy, Ibid., p. 110.

p. 52, "Charlie Chaplin." Wikiquote, Wikipedia. en.wikiquote.org/wiki/Charlie_Chaplin#The_Great_Dictator_.281940.29

Chapter 6

p. 54, par. 2, Duyvendak, J. J. L., translator. *The Book of Lord Shang*, 1928, pp. 98 and 99. classiques.uqac.ca/classiques/duyvendak_jjl/B25_book_of_lord_shang/duyvlord.pdf

p. 57, par. 2, Heiden, Konrad. *Hitler: a Biography*. New York: Knopf, 1936, p. 311.

p. 57, par. 6, Overy, Ibid., p. 179.

p. 57, par. 6, "German Propaganda Archive." Calvin College. www.calvin.edu/academic/cas/gpa/parole.htm

p. 58, Hitler, Adolf. *Mein Kampf*, James Murphy translation. Volume 1, Chapter 10, p. 134. www.adolfhitler.ws/lib/mk/39index.htm

p. 59, par. 1, Overy, Ibid., pp. 178–179.

Chapter 7

p. 60, par. 3, Overy, Ibid., p. 246.

p. 61, par. 7, "Ghetto." Wikipedia. en.wikipedia.org/wiki/Ghetto

p. 63, Ghelpernus, Dimitri. *Kovno Ghetto Diary*. Moscow, Russia: 1948. www. jewishgen.org/Yizkor/kaunas/Kau002.html#preface

p. 64, par. 4, Ferree, Chuck. "Concentration Camp Listing." Jewish Virtual Library. www.jewishvirtuallibrary.org/jsource/Holocaust/cclist.html

p. 64, par. 7–p. 65, par. 1, Schneideman, Leo. "Personal Histories: Camps." Holocaust Personal Histories. www.ushmm.org/museum/exhibit/online/phistories.index.php?content=phi_camps_arrival_uu.htm

p. 65, par. 4, "Holocaust." Wikipedia. en.wikipedia.org/wiki/Holocaust.

p. 65, par. 7, Moyers, Bill. "Welcome to Doomsday." *New York Review of Books.* www.nybooks.com/articles/article-preview?article_id=17852

p. 67, par. 1, Overy, Ibid., 261.

p. 67, par. 4, Quoted in Overy, Ibid., 483.

p. 67, par. 5, Harding, Luke. 'Interview: Erna Flegel." *Guardian Unlimited.* May 2, 2005. www.guardian.co.uk/secondworldwar/story/0,14058,1474705,00.html

Chapter 8

p. 69, par. 4, "Vladimir Lenin." Wikipedia. en.wikipedia.org/wiki/Lenin

p. 73, Overy, Ibid., p. 327.

p. 75, par. 1, Overy, Ibid., p. 39.

Chapter 9

p. 79, par. 2, Cranfield, Cliff. "Russia and the Soviet Union 1917-1945 Stalin." Charles Sturt University. hsc.csu.edu.au/modern_history/national_studies/russia/russia_key_features4/page62.htm#anchor117059.

p. 79, par. 4, Samadoghlu, Vagif. "Stalin's Personality Cult." Azerbiajani International, Autumn 1999. www.azeri.org/Azeri/az_latin/latin_articles/latin_text/latin_73/eng_73/73_stalin_cult.html

p. 80, par. 1, Samadoghlu, Ibid.

p. 80, par. 4–p. 81, par. 1, Avdienko, A. O. "Hymn to Stalin." *Modern History Sourcebook.* www.fordham.edu/halsall/mod/stalin-worship.html

p. 81, par. 4, Kreis, Steven. "The Age of Totalitarianism: Stalin and Hitler." www.historyguide.org/europe/lecture10.html

p. 82, Overy, Ibid., p. 271.

p. 83, par. 3, Overy, Ibid., p. 276.

Chapter 10

p. 85, par. 4, Suny, Ronald. "In the Bedroom (With Stalin)." *The Nation*, September 27, 2004. http://www.thenation.com/doc. mhtml?i=20040927&s=suny

p. 86, par. 2, Arendt, Ibid., pp. 426–427.

p. 86, par. 5, Kreis, Ibid.

p. 86, par. 8–p. 87, par. 1, Arendt, Ibid., p. 445.

p. 87, par. 3, "Genocide in the Twentieth Century." The History Place. www.historyplace.com/worldhistory/genocide/stalin.htm

p. 87, par. 6–p. 88, par. 1, "Ukraine Famine." United Human Rights Council. www.unitedhumanrights.org/Genocide/Ukraine_famine.htm

p. 88, par. 2, Overy, Ibid., p. 345.

p. 88, par. 4, Arendt, Ibid., p. 322.

p. 88, par. 5, "Joseph Stalin." Wikipedia. en.wikipedia.org/wiki/Joseph_Stalin

p. 89, Payne, Robert. *The Rise and Fall of Stalin.* New York: Simon and Schuster, 1965, p. 713.

Chapter 11

p. 92, par. 8–p. 98, par. 1, "Hundred Flowers Campaign." Wikipedia. en.wikipedia.org/wiki/Hundred_Flowers_Campaign

p. 93, par. 1, "Hundred Flowers Campaign," Ibid.

p. 93, par. 7–p. 94, par. 1, Chirot, Ibid., p. 188.

Chapter 12

p. 95, par. 1, Chirot, Ibid., p. 195.

p. 97, par. 1, Chirot, Daniel. *Modern Tyrants*. Princeton, NJ: Princeton University Press, 1994, pp. 195–196.

p.97,par. 4,"RedGuards(China)."QuickSeekEncyclopedia.redguardschina. quickseek.com

p. 98, par. 2, Mao Zedong. *The Little Red Book* Chapter 5. www. morningsun.org/living/redbook/toc.html

p. 98, par. 3, Mao Zedong. *The Little Red Book*, Chapter 2. www. morningsun.org/living/redbook/toc.html

p. 98, par. 4, Mao Zedong. *The Little Red Book*, Chapter 2. www. morningsun.org/living/redbook/toc.html

p. 98, par. 5, Mao Zedong. *The Little Red Book*, Chapter 11. www. morningsun.org/living/redbook/toc.html

p. 98, par. 6, Mao Zedong. *The Little Red Book*, Chapter 31. www. morningsun.org/living/redbook/toc.html

p. 99, par. 1, Nosotro, Rit. "Mao Zedong: Founder of the People's Republic of China." www. hyperhistory.net/apwh/bios/b3maozedong.htm

p. 99, par. 2, Chirot, Ibid., p. 8.

Chapter 13

p. 103, par. 2, Applebaum, Anne. "How Evil Works." *The New Republic*. December 30, 2004. www.tnr.com/user/nregi.mhtml?i=20041227 &s=applebaum122704&pt=pqYvPYsWUY8UiFqGkkRKxw

p. 103, par. 7, "But You Can Call Me Il." *Harper's Magazine*. November 2, 2005. www.harpers.org/ButYouCanCallMeIl.html

p. 103, par. 8–p. 104, par. 1, "Rank Order—Population." *The World Factbook*. www.cia.gov/cia/publications/factbook/rankorder/2119rank.html

p. 104, par. 1, "Background Note: North Korea." U.S. Department of State. www.state.gov/r/pa/ei/bgn/2792.htm.

p. 104, par. 3, Haggard, Stephan and Marcus Noland. *Hunger and Human Rights: The Politics of Famine in North Korea.* Washington D.C.: U.S. Committee for Human Rights in North Korea, 2005. www.hrnk.org/hunger/origins.html

p. 104, par. 6, "Toughs at the Top." *The Economist.* December 16, 2004. www.economist.com/displaystory.cfm?story_id=3445136

p. 104, par. 7, "Starved of Rights: Human Rights and the Food Crisis in the Democratic People's Republic of Korea (North Korea)." *Amnesty International.* January 17, 2004. web.amnesty.org/library/index/engasa240032004

p. 105, par. 6, "List of Dictators." Wikipedia. en.wikipedia.org/wiki/List_of_dictators

p. 106, par. 6, Mueller, Andrew. "The Tyranny of Design." *The Guardian,* October 8, 2005. www.guardian.co.uk/theguide/books/story/0,146841586148,00.html

p. 109, par. 3, Roberts, Marc. "Pillage and Plunder: An Anthology of African Dictators." 2003. www.ssn.flinders.edu.au/global/africa/marcroberts/body.htm

p. 109, par. 6, Tumanov, Boris. "Dictators' Kitchen." *New Times,* June 2006. www.newtimes.ru/eng/detail.asp?art_id=899

p. 110, Maykuth, Andrew. "Congo's Palaces of Excess in Ruins after Mobutu, a City Withers." *Philadelphia Inquirer,* September 22, 2000. www.maykuth.com/Africa/congo922.htm

p. 111, par. 1, "Robert Mugabe Is Poised to Rig a General Election Once Again." *The Economist,* March 23, 2005. www.economist.com/world/africa/displayStory.cfm?story_id=3793417

p. 111, par. 2, Wrong, Micheala. *In the Footsteps of Mr. Kurtz: Living on the Brink of Disaster in Mobutu's Congo.* New York: Harper Perennial, 2002, p. 94.

p. 111, par. 3, "Mobutu Sese Seko." Encarta. encarta.msn.com/encyclopedia_761578969/Mobutu_Sese_Seko.html

Chapter 14

p. 113, par. 1, "Convention on the Prevention and Punishment of the Crime of Genocide." Human Rights Web. www.hrweb.org/legal/genocide.html

p. 113, par. 3, Wong, Edward. "Hussein's Testimony Prompts Closure of Court to Public." *New York Times*, March 15, 2006. www.nytimes.com/2006/03/15/international/middleeast/15cnd-hussein.html?hp&ex=1142485200&en=962231fdb9abeea2&ei=5094&partner=homepage

p. 115, par. 7, Chirot, Ibid., p. 9.

All Internet sites were active and available when this book was sent to press.

Further Information

Books

Blackwood, Alan. *Twenty Tyrants*. New York: Marshall Cavendish, 1990.

Green, Robert. *Dictators*. San Diego, CA: Lucent Books, 2000.

Haugen, Brenda. *Adolf Hitler: Dictator of Nazi Germany.* Mankato, MN: Compass Point Books, 2006.

————. *Joseph Stalin: Dictator of the Soviet Union*. Mankato, MN: Compass Point Books, 2006.

Orwell, George. *Animal Farm*. New York: Signet Classics, 2004.

Scandiffio, Laura. *Evil Masters: The Frightening World of Tyrants*. Toronto, Canada: Annick Press, 2005.

Web Sites

These Web sites are good places to pick up information and ideas on the people, places, events, and ideas discussed in this book.

Asian Revolutions in the Twentieth Century: Mao Zedong
www.exeas.org/asian-revolutions/leaders-mao-zedong-links.html
This valuable Columbia University site contains links to primary source material about Mao and his cult of personality, including posters, photographs, and speeches.

German Propaganda Archive
www.calvin.edu/academic/cas/gpa
A university Web site that contains primary source propaganda documents from Nazi Germany, including posters, cartoons, photos, speeches, and essays.
The History Place
www.historyplace.com
This extensive Web site presents "a fact-based, common sense approach in the presentation of the history of humanity, with great care given to accuracy." It includes a special section on Nazi Germany and World War II.

Holocaust Personal Histories
www.ushmm.org/museum/exhibit/online/phistories/index.php?content=phi_camps_arrival_uu.htm
This site contains primary source material of Holocaust survivors who tell their stories.

Modern Dictators and Human Rights Violations
www.lkwdpl.org/schools/horacemann/dictators/
This middle-school Web site contains numerous links to other sites dealing with twenty modern dictators.

Russia and the Soviet Union, 1917–1941: Stalin
hsc.csu.edu.au/modern_history/national_studies/russia/russia_key_features4/page62.htm#anchor117059
This university Web site examines Stalin's brand of totalitarianism and its impact on Russian society.

Bibliography

Arendt, Hannah. *The Origins of Totalitarianism.* New York: Harvest Books, 1985.

Chang, Jung, and Jon Halliday. *Mao: the Unknown Story.* New York: Knopf, 2005.

Chaplin, Charlie, director. *The Great Dictator,* feature film, 1940.

Chirot, Daniel. *Modern Tyrants.* Princeton, New Jersey: Princeton University Press, 1994.

Davis, Paul K. *100 Decisive Battles from Ancient Times to the Present.* New York: Oxford University Press, 1999.

Hitler, Adolf. *Mein Kampf.* www.hitler.org/writings/Mein_Kampf

Marx, Karl, and Friedrich Engels. *The Communist Manifesto.* www.indepthinfo.com/communist-manifesto/manifest.txt

Orrizio, Riccardo. *Talk of the Devil: Encounters with Seven Dictators.* New York: Walker & Company, 2004.

Overy, Richard. *The Dictators: Hitler's Germany, Stalin's Russia.* New York: W. W. Norton, 2004.

Renais, Alain, director. *Night and Fog,* documentary film, 1955.

Riefenstahl, Leni, director. *Triumph of the Will,* documentary film, 1935.

Wrong, Micheala. *In the Footsteps of Mr. Kurtz: Living on the Brink of Disaster in Mobutu's Congo.* New York: Harper Perennial, 2002.

Zedong, Mao. *The Little Red Book.* www.morningsun.org/living/redbook/toc.html

Index

Page numbers in **boldface** are illustrations, tables, and charts.

About the Author

Ron Fridell has written for radio, TV, newspapers, and textbooks. He has written books on social and political issues, such as terrorism and espionage, and scientific topics, such as DNA fingerprinting and global warming. His most recent book for Marshall Cavendish Benchmark was *Environmental Issues* in our Open for Debate series. He taught English as a second language while a member of the Peace Corp in Bangkok, Thailand. He lives in Tuscon, Arizona, with his wife Patricia and his dog, an Australian Shepherd named Madeline.